KAHLIL GIBRAN

Alexandre Najjar

KAHLIL GIBRAN

Author of *The Prophet*

Translated from the French by
Rae Azkoul

SAQI

London San Francisco Beirut

ISBN: 978-0-86356-668-4

First published in French as *Khalil Gibran* by Pygmalion / Gérard Watrelet in 2002

© Pygmalion / Gérard Watelet, Paris, 2002

This English translation published by Saqi in 2008

Translation © Rae Azkoul, 2008

A full CIP record for this book is available from the British Library.
A full CIP record for this book is available from the Library of Congress.
Manufactured in Lebanon

SAQI

26 Westbourne Grove, London W2 5RH
825 Page Street, Suite 203, Berkeley, California 94710
Tabet Building, Mneimneh Street, Hamra, Beirut
www.saqibooks.com

Contents

Illustrations

Preface

Gibran is an enigma. Since 1923, the year his masterpiece *The Prophet* was published, he has become famous worldwide. In 1996, nine million copies of this cult book were sold in the USA alone by his publisher Alfred A. Knopf. Translated into more than forty languages, *The Prophet* has never ceased to charm readers: in Germany, its success is astounding, and in Italy the paperback has appeared at the top of the best-seller lists. In the 60s, the student and hippy movements adopted the book which claims, without beating around the bush, that 'Your children are not your children. They are the sons and daughters of Life's longing for itself ...'[1] and, even today, it is not uncommon for extracts from *The Prophet* to be read at weddings or baptisms. John F. Kennedy's famous aphorism, 'And so, my fellow Americans, ask not what your country can do for you; ask what you can do for your country,' echoes Gibran's 'Are you a politician who asks what his country can do for him? ... Or are you a zealous and enthusiastic politician ... who asks himself what he can do for his country?' Even the Beatles were not insensitive to the work of this Lebanese writer,

---

1. Alexander Sutherland Neill placed this sentence by Gibran as an epigraph in his famous book *The Free Children of Summerhill*, published in 1960. Neill's thesis was a protest against a social system interested in instructing, rather than educating, children..

as evidenced in John Lennon's lyrics to *Julia*, clearly inspired by the author.

Aside from the monuments dedicated to the artist in Lebanon, his native country (the Gibran Museum in Bsharri and a square in central Beirut, inaugurated in 2001), scattered here and there are plaques, statues and commemorative places paying tribute to his memory. In the USA there is one in Copley Square in Boston and another in Washington, inaugurated on 24 May 1991 by George Bush. On that occasion, in Bush's address, he referred to Gibran as a symbol of peace; 'Part poet, part philosopher, he extracted "the secret of the sea from a drop of dew." Poetry was the language in which he explored his soul and taught us about ours ... He drew us where we were unused to climb and shared what he saw – the promise of a kinder, gentler world.' The prestigious Metropolitan Museum of Art in New York, the Fogg Art Museum, the Boston Museum of Fine Arts, the Newark Museum, the Telfair Museum of Art in Savannah, Georgia ... all of these museums exhibit works by Gibran, and the Lebanese community in Brazil has inaugurated a cultural centre simply called 'Gibran'.

And yet ... and yet Gibran is omitted from most Western literary handbooks and anthologies. Why is that? This ostracism, according to Amin Maalouf, a renowned Lebanese author who writes in French, is due to the fact that *The Prophet* cannot be classified or labelled. It is neither a poem, nor a novel, nor an essay. It fits into no well-defined category. And its author is just as elusive. He was an Arab writer who wrote in English, was born in Lebanon, and was raised in the USA. He straddles both sides of the fence, one foot in the East and one in the West. Gibran is not part of the mainstream.

Numerous books and articles have been written about him, but are they exhaustive? Surely not. The records of his correspondence are not complete. One of his relatives in the USA, the sculptor and his namesake, Kahlil Gibran, is probably still in possession of some documents that have not yet surfaced. The present book sheds light on some information previously unknown or previously misconstrued, like the letters from Gibran to Helena Ghostine, the archives of his publisher Alfred A. Knopf and the legal proceedings against his family, but it does not claim to be exhaustive. Its purpose is to retrace the path of the artist with a simplicity similar to the simplicity of his writing, with excerpts to reinforce it, to render as clear as possible a thought that many sought to complicate, no doubt to give his work a philosophical dimension that he himself did not seek. 'Things are said simply, with authority.' That was Gibran's rule of thumb. That will be ours too.

ONE

Bsharri

*T*o the east of the Mediterranean Sea, at the crossroads of the three continents and three religions, in the north of Lebanon, lies Bsharri. As if emanating from an incense burner, a thick mist drifts up the valley. To the rhythm of the *nay* (a reed flute used in oriental music) played by a shepherd lost in the pasture, the mist climbs up the rocks, implanting itself between the oaks and the cypress trees, and lays itself to rest atop the red-tile-roofed houses. But it would take more than that to subdue the village. The indomitable Bsharri has the same tenacity as its sons, with their tanned complexions and imposing moustaches; it is as resistant as the Cedars of God – Arz el Rab – which stand erect, a heartbeat away, proud and robust in spite of their tilted peaks.

It is these same cedars that inspired the French poet Alphonse de Lamartine to write one of the most beautiful passages in his *Voyage to the East*, 'These trees are the most famous natural monuments in the world. Religion, poetry, and history have paid tribute to them as well. These are divine beings in the form of trees.' Baptized 'Buissera' by the Crusaders, who turned it into one of their fiefs in the county of Tripoli, Bsharri, at the end of the nineteenth century, loomed like an austere village in the middle of a tormented landscape. Lamartine was not mistaken when in his last traveller's notebook he noted, 'The village of Beschierai, where the houses can barely be distinguished from the rocks surrounding them ... One has to get down there on a path embedded in rocks so steep that one cannot imagine anyone attempting the descent ...'

Old photographs[1] reveal one particular spot suspended between sky and earth, traditional dwellings huddled one against another, forming a protective cover from the invader, be it the harsh winter or the Ottoman. The Ottoman was the enemy, always the enemy, despite the fact that the area had enjoyed a certain autonomy since the arrival of the French troops under the command of General Marquis de Beaufort d'Hautpoul in 1860. It became one of the *mutassarefiat* controlled by an Ottoman subject, a *mutassaref*, appointed by the Turkish authorities and accountable to Istanbul. The Christians of the north, however, refused to collaborate with the foreign governor because having the Bekaa Valley and the coastline cities of Beirut, Tripoli and Sidon[2] amputated from the Lebanese heartland did not sit well with them.

Not far from there is the sacred Qadisha Valley, considered by the Tharaud brothers as 'the valley of Maronite sanctity par excellence ... on the peaks, the cliffs, the valley floor, or well engraved in the rocks, one can see nothing but churches, chapels, monasteries, and cells. An entire mystical life is attached to the undergrowth, suspended over the precipice ...'[3] Who are these Maronites who lived, and still live, in this sacred place? It was at the end of the fourth century, near Antioch, that a recluse saint named Maroun became known for his

1.   Ghazi Geagea, Bsharri, Beirut 1999.
2.   Kamal Salibi, *The History of Lebanon*, Naufal, 1988, pp. 207 and 213.
3.   Jérôme and Jean Tharaud, *Le Chemin de Damas*, Plon 1923, quoted by H. Mallat in *L'Académie française et le Liban*, Dar an-Nahar 2001, p. 253.

erudition, the austerity of his lifestyle, and his gift for performing miracles.[1] Acknowledged by Saint John Chrysostom, he became the spiritual leader of a group of hermits, who, at his death around 410 AD, founded the nucleus of the Maronite Church and built a monastery in his honour on the bank of the Orontes. Persecuted from the seventh century onwards, the Maronites took refuge in the mountains of North Lebanon, and during the Crusades they offered invaluable services to the Franks. Their church was affiliated to Rome, where in 1584 Pope Gregory XIII founded the Collegium Maronitorium, using Syriac, the Aramaic dialect spoken by Christ, in the liturgy. There are currently approximately four million followers of this Church. Their numbers are not limited to Lebanon, the country of the Cedars, where St Maroun's Day is celebrated on 9 February each year. Maronites can also be found in Cyprus, Rhodes and other countries hosting the Lebanese diaspora.

The most striking spot in this valley is undoubtedly the Monastery of Saint Anthony of Qoshaya,[2] known for having one of the first printing presses in the East and where it was, until the last century, common practice to chain madmen to rocks in a deep, dark cave at the entrance of the monastery in the belief that their demons would be exorcised. As if madness were heresy.

> *Give me the nay and sing.*
> *Singing is the secret to eternity,*
> *And the plaintiveness of the nay lingers*
> *After the end of existence.*
>
> *Do you, like me,*
> *Prefer the forest to the castles*

---

1. Mgr Pierre Dib, *Histoires des Maronites*, 2nd edn, Librarie Orientale, 2004, vol. I, p. 4; Mgr. Saïd Saïd, *Les Eglises orientales et leurs droits*, Cariscript 1989, p. 55; J-P. Valognes, *Vie et mort des Chrétiens d'Orient*, Fayard 1994, p. 368.
2. Originally a Syriac expression meaning 'the treasure of life'.

As a dwelling place,
To follow the streams
And climb the rocks?

Do you bathe in the fragrance
And dry yourself in the light?
Do you intoxicate yourself in the dawn
Of the ether-filled cups?

Do you, like me, sit in the twilight
Among the vine leaves
With grapes suspended
Like golden chandeliers?

Do you, like me, sleep in the grass
At night, taking the sky for your cover,
Giving up the future
And forgetting the past?

Give me the nay and sing,
Forgetting ills and remedies
As men are but lines written
Only in water.[1]

It is in this setting, glorified so well in his poems, that Gibran Khalil Gibran was born on 6 January 1883.[2] His father, Khalil Saad Gibran, a tax collector for his county, used to spend most of his days drinking and playing cards. He was originally from a Maronite family in Syria, who during the sixteenth century came to Baalbeck before moving to Bshile and finally settling in Bsharri. 'He had a domineering

---

1.   This excerpt from *Processions* by Gibran was magnificently sung by the Lebanese diva, Feyrouz.

2.   An unpublished letter by Gibran to Blanche Knopf dated 11 March 1928 confirms this previously debatable date (see also letter of 6 January 1906 to J. Peabody and letter of 11 January 1921 to May Ziadeh).

temperament and was not a loving person,' recollected Gibran, who suffered from his father's lack of understanding and his bullying.

Gibran's mother, Kamila Rahmeh, was very dark, fine-looking, and had a beautiful voice which she had inherited from her father. She was the daughter of Father Istiphan Rahmeh, and she married Khalil after the death of her first husband and the annulment of her second marriage to Yusuf Elias Geagea. She had a son, Boutros, born in 1877, by the former, who had died in Brazil, where together they had gone to seek their fortune.

Kamila watched lovingly over her four children. She had two daughters, Mariana and Sultana, born in 1885 and 1887 respectively. She struggled to give them a good education and loved telling them stories and Lebanese legends. In a letter to his cousin Nakhli, dated 27 September 1910, Gibran reminisces about these exquisite moments. 'Do you remember the interesting tales we used to listen to, sitting around the hearth, on the cold, rainy days when the snow fell outside and the wind blew among the houses?'

Thanks to his mother, Gibran learned Arabic, took an interest in music and drawing, and discovered the Bible. In her company, he went to church every Sunday, attended mass celebrated according to the Maronite liturgy, and tried to learn the litany in Syriac, even though it was incomprehensible to him. Sensing that her son was artistically inclined, Kamila gave him a book of Leonardo da Vinci's collected works. For Gibran it was a revelation. He was speechless, in awe of the great power of the Italian painter. He later recalled, 'I never got over the feeling somewhere in the recesses of my soul that part of his spirit was lodged in my own. I was a child when I saw the drawings of this amazing man for the first time. I will never forget that moment as long as I live. It was as if a ship lost in the fog had suddenly found a compass.'

Deeply influenced by his mother, the future writer pays homage to her in *Broken Wings*: 'The most beautiful word on the lips of mankind is "mother", and the most beautiful call is the call "my mother". It is a word full of hope and love, a sweet and kind word coming from the depths of the heart. The mother is everything – she is our consolation in sorrow, our hope in misery, and our strength in weakness. She is the source of love, mercy, sympathy and forgiveness. He who loses his mother loses a pure soul who blesses and guards him constantly.'

When his mother died, Gibran wrote to his cousin Nakhli in Bsharri, 'About the clothes you found in the trunk of my late mother, even though they have no great value and contain nothing very precious, my deepest desire is to keep most of them. I consecrate the memory of my mother and treasure her belongings.' And to May Ziadeh, his friend in Cairo, he confessed, 'Ninety percent of my character and disposition are inherited from my mother, except that I cannot claim to have her sweetness, gentleness, and generosity.'

Gibran's first years were carefree, despite the parental quarrels he witnessed and a serious fall he took while walking along a cliff with his cousin. The accident resulted in a dislocated shoulder, which forced him to lie on a plank with his arms crossed for forty days.

The boy came to the attention of a local doctor and poet, Selim Daher,[1] who took him under his wing. Gibran never forgot him. After Daher's death in 1912, Gibran wrote his heartfelt condolences to the family, 'His talents and good qualities were unique ... I owe him the moral awakening, which thanks to his love and sympathy, left an impact on my adolescence.' And in a eulogy written on 22 July 1912, he called on his fellow countrymen not to cry over 'the Son of the Cedars' as 'death renews the days of he who confronts it with a noble and beautiful soul, and it puts him back on his feet facing the sun ...'

---

1.   Daher was born in 1865 in Bsharri, studied at the Collège de la Sagesse, and in 1887 received his medical diploma from the American University of Beirut.

At first, Gibran went to the Monastery of Mar Licha, where Father Germanos inculcated the foundations of Arabic and Syriac in him. He was then enrolled in the primary school of Bsharri, run by Father Semaan, who taught him how to read and write. There are many anecdotes about this period, but they are legendary and therefore difficult to verify. One of them is about a day on which the priest made Gibran copy out a Syriac lesson (that he had failed to learn) ten times. He approached his pupil's desk to monitor the work, only to find him drawing a sleeping donkey with a black skullcap over its head! His friend, Mikhail Naimy, reported that the little Gibran had used a piece of charcoal to trace his first drawings on walls. He also recounts that one Good Friday Gibran was found at the village cemetery with a bouquet of cyclamen in his hands. He was too young to go with the other village children to gather flowers to place at the crucifix in church during the mass. Left to his own devices, he mysteriously disappeared, causing his parents much anguish. 'When I arrived at church to place the flowers that I had picked myself, I found the gate closed,' he later explained to his mother, 'so I went to the cemetery to look for Christ's tomb!' Barbara Young, his companion in his final days, reported that Gibran had told her that when he was four, he 'planted paper in the earth and waited for it to germinate'.

Gibran grew up in a conservative society. He quickly distinguished himself with his artistic potential and unbridled imagination, all of which led his friends to think of him as a dreamer. His fertile imagination was both a blessing for Gibran the writer – his entire work is nourished with symbols and allegories – and a curse for Gibran the man, insofar as one can disassociate the writer from the man. Like so many artists, Gibran was narcissistic. At times he was conceited and talked about himself in the third person. He resorted to his imagination to compensate for his own weaknesses. Like many Easterners, he had a natural propensity for embellishing stories and fantasising. To suit the circumstances and sometimes for no reason whatsoever, he did not hesitate to distort reality. His fabrications included his having been born in Bombay, India; that the romantic ballads he wrote during his childhood became popular in Syria and Egypt; that he was the disciple of Auguste Rodin; and that he fell victim to an attempt on his life by the Ottomans in Paris. How can one hold this against him? How many writers invent other lives, casting themselves in roles that don't even resemble their own? Emulating Hemingway, Swift, Yeats or Malraux, he created, or recreated, his own character as novelists do. Isn't this the poetic licence to which every writer has recourse, in the same way that the writer recreates the story itself? The renowned quotation, 'I rape Truth, but I father beautiful children,' attributed to Alexander Dumas, exemplifies this notion. Is it not the same as to create imaginary settings like Rabelais or Jules Verne did? In an interview in *Le Monde*, Robbe-Grillet said, 'For an autobiography, it doesn't bother me in the least to invent things transformed by my memory.' People talk of 'white lies' when they refer to harmless untruths of no consequence. 'I have told many lies in my life, but I have never been dishonest,' wrote Gibran. If Gibran happened to lie, it was only to tell a 'white lie'.

In the midst of nature, Gibran spent happy days in the company of his half-brother and his two sisters. He loved storms, which swept the region in winter and later inspired his painting 'Tempest', the title of a book, *The Tempests*, and various other texts. In a letter to May Ziadeh, he wrote, 'We are having a terrible snow storm today. You know how much I love storms, and especially snow storms!' And in another letter to Mary Haskell, 'The great storm, for which I have been waiting, has just come. The sky is black. The sea is white with foam, and the spirits of some unknown gods are flying between the sky and the sea ... Mary, what is there in a storm that moves me so? Why am I so much better and stronger and more certain of life while a storm is passing? I do not know, and yet I love a storm more, far more than anything in nature.'

Gibran was 'impregnated' with the magical spectacle of the surrounding landscape, from the Holy Valley to Baalbeck and from the sea, which he discovered for the first time when he was eight, to Marjhine in the Hermel, where his father owned a farm and where in the summer he found his Muslim friends Ahmad Allaou and Sadek Allam.[1] He stored images in his memory, which later populated his poetic universe. Can one say enough about the influence of Bsharri on Gibran? Everything: the sun, the storms, the shepherds, the wheat, the myrtle, the mist, the wind, the streams, the 'secret hills and songs of the forest', the plough, the flute, the reed, the gesticulations of the villagers who were selling, folding, sifting their merchandise ... all of these images are inherent in each one of his books, and in particular in *The Prophet*, where all the symbols find their origins in the imagery of the author's native village. Even towards the end of his life, in *The Wanderer*, Gibran continued to use familiar settings for his parables: the city of Bsharri for 'The Three Gifts', the Qadisha Valley for 'The River', and the slopes of Mount Lebanon for 'The Quest'. His attachment to the world of his childhood was visceral. The almost constant backdrop of his visual work is the landscape resembling Bsharri: uneven mountains with pink and blue hues, massive rocks, deep valleys, and springs ... Pictures like 'Dance and Rhythm', 'The Gift', 'Birth of Tragedy' or 'Woman Discovering Nature' are a perfect reconstruction of this environment which the little Gibran came to know.

> I, myself, he wrote in *Broken Wings*, recollect the beautiful region in the North of Lebanon and, as soon as I close my eyes on the ocean which separates me from my homeland, I see

---

1. Fouad E. Boustani, *al-Fousoul*, summer 1981, no. 7; Henri Zogheib, 'With Gibran in Marjhine,' *an-Nahar*, 15 and 17 October 2001.

these valleys filled with magic and majesty, these mountains with their glory and nobility reaching towards the sky; as soon as I make myself deaf to the uproar that fills this society in exile, I hear the murmur of streams and the rustling of the leaves. I long to see again all this beauty of which I speak just as a newborn longs to see his mother's breast.

Gradually, the child learned that 'tolerance is love sick with the sickness of haughtiness.' In a country where various religious communities lived together (Pope John Paul II said that Lebanon was 'a message') he discovered the meaning of coexistence, the acceptance of the 'other'. The Lebanese writer Marun Abbud's accurate perception of Lebanon ran along these lines:

> All the peoples of the earth have passed through this land. They fought battles and then departed, leaving behind traces of their cultural heritage, which combine to form the fabric of our way of thinking. There is no other nation on earth that can claim such an interlacing of thoughts. Look. In Lebanon you can find convents and temples, fortresses and citadels, churches, cathedrals, mosques, amphitheaters, and stadiums. On each peak stands a convent, on each hill you can find a temple or a fortress, and in each valley a fortified refuge.

One morning, a Greek Orthodox travelling salesman of olive oil was sent packing by a Bsharri woman because he was a non-Maronite. Incensed by her prejudice, Gibran's father bought oil from the poor merchant and invited him into his home for supper, much to the delight of his son. This anecdote is undoubtedly proof enough that sectarianism, merely a more politically correct expression of fanaticism, was alien to the Gibrans who were, unlike other Lebanese families, still scarred by the bloody conflicts between the Druze and the Christians in 1860, as many still are, in our days, by a civil war lasting fifteen years. Inevitably, the Gibrans would learn more about tolerance when they became expatriates, as then they would need to seek acceptance from a society foreign to them.

Throughout his life, out of nostalgia for his country and his childhood, Gibran would delve voluptuously back into his past. Convinced that 'remembrance is a kind of encounter,' he missed no opportunity to share the images that he kept of this blessed era with his Lebanese friends.

> When I was a child, all the villagers used to gather at the church on Christmas Eve. The snow was deep and silent. Lanterns in hand, we walked through the night ... At midnight, the bells along with the voices of the elders and children rose up in an old hymn of Galilee. The steeple of the little chapel seemed to reach the sky.

To his cousin Nakhli in Brazil he also wrote:

> Reading between the lines, I perceive the phantoms of your affections, as if they come from Brazil to restore to my heart the echo of the valleys, the mountains, and the rivulets surrounding Bsharri. Life, my dear Nakhlé, is like the seasons of the year ... Will the spring of our life ever return to us so we may be happy again with the trees, smiling with the flowers, running with the brooks, and singing with the birds, like we used to do when Boutros was still alive? Will the tempest that separated us ever reunite us? Will we ever go back to Bsharri and sit by the Mar Girgis Church? ... Our souvenirs hover over the places where we once knew joy. I am one of those who remember such places regardless of distance or time, and I do not allow a single souvenir to be extinguished. It is my everlasting remembrance of the past that causes my sorrow sometimes. Yet, if I had to choose between joy and sorrow, I would not exchange the chagrin of my heart for the joys of the whole world.

On 28 March 1908 in Boston, he evokes the memories of his childhood in a letter sent to his friend Amin Gorayeb, editor and owner of *al-Mohajer*, the daily Arabic newspaper published in New York.

> Remember me when you see the sun rising from behind Mount Sannine or Fam el Mizab. Think of me when you see the sun beginning its slow descent into sunset, spreading its red garment over the mountains and the valleys as if it was shedding blood instead of tears as it bids Lebanon farewell. Recall my name when you see the shepherds sitting in the shade of the trees, blowing their reeds, and filling the silent fields with their soothing music, like Apollo did when he was exiled to this world. Think of me when you see the young ladies carrying the earthenware water jugs on their shoulders. Remember me when you see the Lebanese villager plowing the earth, before the face of the sun, with beads of perspiration adorning his forehead while his back is bent under the heavy duty of labor. Remember me when you hear the chants and hymns that Nature has woven from the sinews of moonlight, mingled with the aromatic scent of the valleys, mixed with the frolicsome breeze of the Holy Cedars and poured into the heart of the Lebanese.

And then on 18 February 1913:

> Take a walk in the morning, stand at the summit of one of the Lebanese mountains, and reflect on the sun when it is rising and dispersing its golden rays on the villages and valleys. Let these heavenly pictures remain etched in your heart so that we can share them with you when you return!

The writer's attachment to his native land, undoubtedly exacerbated by his absence, finds its most striking illustration in *Jesus, the Son of Man*, where Christ's face is compared to the rocky peaks of Lebanon, where Christ chose his disciples among the people of the

North and the slopes of Lebanon and asks that Lebanese snow be his shroud. In fact, could Gibran have been this 'bridge' between the East and the West had he not been Lebanese? Surely not. The open-mindedness and receptiveness of the Lebanese towards the rest of the world, no doubt encouraged by trade, emigration and numerous missions established throughout the country; seventeen civilizations succeeded on their soil; their propensity to assimilate others' ideas: all these converged in Gibran. In an article published in 1947 in *Le Figaro* entitled 'A Window Between Two Worlds', the French author Georges Duhamel wrote:

> Lebanon is a place where osmosis takes place in the middle of an invisible and all too often impervious membrane separating two human societies. In one of his works, Kipling said "East is East and West is West and never the twain shall meet." The traveller who pays close attention to Lebanese society must know that Kipling was mistaken. The union of which he despaired, which one can indeed despair of at times, can perhaps be designed in Lebanon first.[1]

It is not surprising, therefore, to read this inscription on the base of Gibran's statue in the heart of Beirut: 'If Lebanon had not been my native country, I would have chosen it to be!'

❧❦❧

In 1891, Gibran's life changed dramatically. His father was arrested for mismanagement of the tax money he collected. Kamila protested her husband's innocence in vain. The verdict was pronounced with no room for appeal: he was sentenced and stripped of all his assets. 'Property, orchards and fields, as well as the family house with all its

---

1. Quoted by H. Mallat, in *L'Académie française et le Liban*, Dar an-Nahar 2001, p. 261. The famous quotation by Kipling is taken from 'The Ballad of East and West' in *Sixty Poems*, p. 97.

contents including valuables, books and furniture, many of which were heirlooms. Everything was confiscated,' reported Gibran. 'My father was taken to Beirut, where he was incarcerated.' Kamila was wholly distressed. What were they to do? Where were they to go? How was she going to feed four children when she had no income? Her instinct was to consider emigration. Many of her compatriots, spurred by the economic crisis and by the ever-escalating and crippling taxes, had gone to find refuge under more clement skies. It is estimated that between 1860 and 1914 there were 330,000 Lebanese who left the ports of Beirut and Tripoli for the American continent.[1] Some struck it rich; others, like her first husband, never came back. She made up her mind, but where was she going to find money for the trip? She sold the precious items she had inherited from her father and the utensils spared by her husband's creditors, solicited the intervention of a bishop with the American authorities to obtain permission to emigrate, and received a letter of recommendation from the American University of Beirut (then called 'Syrian College') to facilitate the necessary formalities.[2]

In 1895 the family took a ship to their destination in the New World: Boston, where in 1854 the first Lebanese immigrant had disembarked as if landing on the moon.

1. Elia Safa, *L'Émigration Libanaise*, St Joseph University, Beirut 1960. Certain demographers quote the figures at 217,000 (A. Atat. 'Emigration et diaspora libanaise dans le monde', *Défense nationale libanaise*, October 2001, p. 40)..

2. Antoine Ghattas Karam, *La vie et l'œuvre littéraire de Gibran Khalil Gibran*, Dar an-Nahar 1981, p. 18; Jean-Pierre Dahdah, *Gibran, une biographie*, Albin Michel, 1994, p. 68.

TWO

Off to the New World

*O*n 17 June 1895 Kamila and her children disembarked at Ellis Island.[1] The young Gibran was twelve years old and had a lot to learn about the 'civilisation on wheels'. Barbara Young, his biographer, reported on his first memory there. 'It was the night he spent at Old Brevoort House, on Fifth Avenue and Eighth Street in New York City. He wandered around the next day, riding all along the avenue in an old horse-and-carriage and then returned to the hotel.'

Soon afterwards, the family arrived in Boston. Boston! The cradle of some of the greatest causes in American history: the revolution for independence, the abolition of slavery, and the emancipation of women. Considered the 'lighthouse' of New England and inhabited by half a million people at the time, Boston was the historical capital of the United States. It was only a short distance away from the port where the *Mayflower*, carrying the 102 colonists fleeing England, had disembarked.

Lebanese and Syrians lived in the South End neighbourhood in

---

1.   Robin Waterfield found their exact date of arrival in the New York office of the National Archives, Northeastern section, as published in *Prophet: The Life and Times of Kahlil Gibran*, 1998, p. 10.

precarious conditions. At first, the Gibrans took shelter with relatives who had left Bsharri for Boston five years earlier. Later on, they settled on the fifth floor of a dilapidated building at 9 Oliver Place[1] next to Beach Street. The hovel they lived in was dark, the din from the street replaced the soft music of the cascading sacred valley, and its noxious odours emanated from neighbouring sewers infested with flies and stray dogs. But no matter! One had to survive. Meanwhile, their father back home was sending them little money, the amount dwindling with each instalment.

The eldest in the family, Boutros, aged eighteen, set about looking for work and soon found a job in a textile shop. The young man had perseverance and was determined to earn enough money to provide his step-brother with an education and his mother and step-sisters with peace of mind. As for Kamila, she followed in the footsteps of most of her fellow expatriates: lugging a bundle on her back, she went door to door selling house linen, lace and Syrian-made silk. Not only did she have to contend with bad weather, but she sometimes also had to bear the humiliation of being turned away as if she were a pest. Later on, she gave this up and devoted herself to sewing. Initially she was helped by Sultana and Mariana, who later went on to become salesgirls in Boutros's shop.

Driven by the will to give shape to his destiny by acquiring knowledge, Gibran attended the local school of Quincy, in the Syrian quarter of town. It was a school where Arab, Jewish, Chinese and East European students studied side by side. In this melting pot typical of the US, he rediscovered tolerance. He was taught to read and write English. His teacher noticed his penchant for literature and presented him with a copy of *Uncle Tom's Cabin*. She encouraged him to draw and introduced him to a local artist who promised him a bright future. It was she who suggested dropping his first name 'Gibran' and moving the

---

1. This neighbourhood is now located in Chinatown.

letter 'h' in his other name. She found that if he signed 'Kahlil Gibran'[1] it would look less obtrusive. The adolescent accepted, and from that moment on, that is how he became known in the United States.

Gibran spent two and a half years at the local Quincy school, of which he kept fond memories. 'My first two years in Boston were the most miserable. My only haven was with my teachers, who were extremely kind to me. Long after I left the school, they continued to write asking about me.'

Saddened to see Boutros killing himself trying to support the family while Gibran spent his time reading, drawing, and daydreaming, Kamila urged Gibran to help his brother out. But the adolescent categorically refused, claiming that 'The little finger of an artist is worth a thousand merchants – except Boutros. One page of poetry is worth all the textiles in the shops of the world.' True to his word, Gibran did not let slip any opportunity to become more cultured. He attended a charitable institution named Denison House, where Catholic priests taught and where drawing and theatre classes were held. He drew a picture of *The Bacchante*, the 'scandalous' statue of Frederick MacMonnies (which sits majestically in the cloisters of the Boston Public Library). He showed the sketch to Florence Pierce, his teacher at Denison House, who was impressed by his talent and introduced him to an influential social worker, Jessie Fremont Beale. On 25 November 1896, Beale wrote to her friend, Fred Holland Day, to suggest that he take the promising young boy under his patronage.

> My dear Mr Day:
> ... I am wondering if you may happen to have an artist friend who would care to become interested in a little Assyrian[2] boy

---

1.   The exact name in Arabic is 'Gibran Khalil Gibran', Khalil being the father's name, which is traditionally used as a middle name in Arabic. In his Arabic works, Gibran signed his full name; in his English works, he abided by his teacher's suggestion.
2.   Beale meant 'Syrian'. The word 'Syria' meant a geographic area (including Syria,

Kahlil G—. He is not connected with any society, so anyone befriending the little chap would be entirely free to do with him what would seem in their judgment wise. He strolled into a drawing class at the College Settlement on Tyler Street last winter and showed a sufficient ability to make Miss Pierce feel that he was capable of some day earning his living in a better way than by selling matches or newspapers on the street, if someone would only help him to get an artistic education.

His future will certainly be that of a street fakir if something is not done for him at once. The family are horribly poor, living at Oliver Place, and will insist upon having some financial assistance from this little boy just as soon as the law will allow unless he is on the road to something better. Next year he will be fourteen, beyond the school age, so we are specially interested to start the little fellow this year in his drawing, if such a thing is at all possible ...

I fear you will feel this request in regard to Kahlil almost an intrusion, but I am so interested in the little fellow myself, and yet so utterly helpless, that I feel as if I must try to find someone else who can be of real use to him.

Born in 1864 in South Dedham, Massachusetts, Fred Holland Day held a special place in the artistic world of his day.[1] He was a bold photographer who used symbolism and mysticism in his works. This dandy was the director of the Copeland & Day Publishing Co., established in Boston in 1893. Among other works, Copeland & Day published the American edition of Oscar Wilde's daring *Salome*. Day had blond hair, a pointed beard, an aquiline nose and light eyes. He donned round spectacles, a black hat with a wide brim, and a cloak. A notorious homosexual, he took interest in the male body and did not hesitate to photograph young Adonises in their skimpiest clothing.

Lebanon, Palestine and Jordan) and did not correspond to any political entity.

1.   In 2001 an exhibition of Holland Day's work was held at the Van Gogh Museum in Amsterdam, and a book written by Pam Roberts was dedicated to the occasion, which included three of his photographs of Gibran.

As Day needed Oriental models for his photographs, he agreed to meet Gibran and gave him an appointment in his studio at 9 Pinckey Street on 9 December 1896. Captivated by this young, dark-complexioned, long-black-haired teenager with a brooding air and a pensive look, Day invited Gibran to pose for him dressed in Arabic, Levantine or Indian clothing. Whether candidly or to satisfy his curiosity, Gibran accepted. *Young Sheikh*, *Kahlil* and *Syrian Boy* were among some of the photographs that Day, fuelled by his fantasies, took of the young model. 'Day has a series of photographs of me. He was very affectionate towards me,' recalled Gibran, and he encouraged all the members of his family to pose for his protector. Day bought him new clothes and invited him to several banquets.

He introduced him to the writing and artwork of William Blake. Gibran was not only overwhelmed by the mythological and prophetic universe of Blake, but also dazzled by the diversity of the sources which enriched his poetic and visual vocabulary. He was sensitive to the abundant symbolism of the works marked by the spiritual dialectic between Good and Evil, between Heaven and Hell, between Regeneration and Disintegration[1] and the attempt 'to open the immortal human eye inward'.[2] Although too young to be able to interpret Blake's thoughts in their entirety, he assimilated some of his critiques of society and the state, including the rebellion against the prince and the priest, the creative virtue of desire, and the supremacy of the imagination linked to an internal God. He also understood, at least in part, the notion of the union of the being and the power of Christ, whom he considered a rebel. Inspired by the great English artist, he began to sketch drawings imbued with symbolism. From that moment on, Gibran was haunted by William Blake, who forever after occupied a special place in his spiritual consciousness.

1.   Henry Lemaitre, *William Blake, Vision and Poetry*, José Corti, 1985, p. 10.
2.   William Blake, *Jerusalem, the Emanation of the Giant* Albion, vol. I, p. 5.

Day also introduced the young Lebanese boy to Swinburne, Carpenter, Whitman, Keats, Emerson and the Romantic writers. Upon Day's recommendation, Gibran read *Treasury of the Humble* by Maurice Maeterlinck, a work in which the author, with moral and philosophical considerations, scrutinised the secrets of inner life. 'Between the ages of fourteen and eighteen, I idolized [Maeterlinck],' remarked Gibran. Maeterlinck, winner of the Nobel Prize for literature in 1911, was a 'magician of mystery' that Day himself photographed in 1901. Gibran was so observant and assimilated what he was taught so well that details revealed in the photos of his mentor, like a crystal ball placed behind the models, figured later in his own works of art.

The impact Day had on Gibran proved to be great. The art of portrait photography plied by his mentor fascinated the young man so much that he experimented with it in his own paintings. He found the liberation from all constraints, the seeking of beauty in the nude and the return to mythology exhilarating. The concern over building bridges between disparate cultures, the permanent quest for spirituality through symbols and Day's 'The indefinite is the road to the infinite' – all of these left their imprint on the young Gibran, who, being so young, was still quite impressionable.

Day opened many doors for Gibran who illustrated several books published by Copeland & Day, among which was the anthology of poetry by the Canadian Duncan Campbell Scott and a book about the astronomer and poet, Omar Khayyam, written by Nathan Haskell Dole. Gradually, Gibran gained ground. One of his illustrations was included in an English translation of Maeterlinck's *Wisdom and Destiny*.

In February 1898, Fred Holland Day organised an exhibition of 250 photographs at the Camera Club in New York, followed by another one in March at the same club in Boston. 'There I met a great many fine people. It was an event and mother dressed me with special care ... I met Miss Peabody, too, who told me that she could see me everywhere. To my great surprise, I had found seven or eight studies of myself, mounted and framed on the walls,' reported Gibran, proud that although barely fifteen years old, some of his works were displayed alongside those of one of the greatest photographers of his time.

Who was Josephine Preston Peabody? Nicknamed 'Posy', this young, refined girl of twenty-three came from a well-to-do family whose business had declined and lost most of its wealth after the death of her father in 1884. She pursued her education in reputable institutions of higher learning, Boston Girls' Latin School and Radcliffe College. She dabbled in poetry and dreamed of being published by Copeland & Day. When she met Gibran at the exhibition in Boston, she asked him, 'I see you everywhere. But you look so sad – why are you sad?'

Gibran was overcome by the beauty of the young woman with pallid skin, magnificent eyes, the neck of a swan and delicate features. He did not deny being sad and by his own admission, he records that 'Mrs. Day said to her son, "I like that young man very much, but I don't like being around him; he never smiles." And it is true. I rarely smiled.' Gibran scrutinised Posy, memorised her features, and promised to draw her portrait as soon as he could.

Gibran's family began to grow concerned about his social life. After all, Day had a fiendish reputation, and people were asking questions. Why was he so attached to this talented but naïve adolescent? Some biographers, basing themselves on this dubious friendship and on the strained relationships Gibran had with women, suspected Gibran of homosexuality. The writer's intransigent attitude towards homosexuality, as confirmed by letters he wrote, and his various affairs, public or secret, with older women, however, render this theory unlikely.

Matters got worse when in February 1897 Gibran fell under the spell of a thirty-year-old woman, the wife of a businessman. Kamila and Boutros were shocked by his behaviour and exasperated by his frequent nocturnal absences. Kamila had opened a shop of Oriental goods at 61 Beach Street, and thanks to her own savings combined with her elder son's, they were able to take action. They had to keep the adolescent away from the frivolous woman and, more importantly, from the influence of Fred Holland Day, who took pictures of naked men! The only solution was to send Gibran back to Lebanon. He accepted unflinchingly.

> It was like a dream, not a clear and pleasant one, but a confusing dream filled with uncertainty. I was leaving my mother, my brother, and my two sisters behind in Boston. But ahead of me, far away in Mount Lebanon, near the Cedars, lay my father. And me? I knew I could only become what I was to be if I went back home.

Although she feared he was making a mistake, his teacher, Florence Pierce, was confident that now Gibran had recognised his artistic tendencies, he could renew the local colouring and return revitalised by a visit to his homeland.

Before leaving, Gibran completed Posy's portrait and, on Fred Holland Day's suggestion, he sent it to the young woman with a dedication. A few days later, Josephine Peabody, who was about to publish her first book with Copeland & Day, received the portrait with a mysterious note in Arabic attached to it. She wrote to Day, 'Indeed I had not forgotten Gibran; but I am much astonished that he should have remembered me.' Intrigued, she consulted a professor of Oriental languages at Harvard for a translation of the dedication. He had modestly written, 'To the dear and esteemed stranger, Josephine Peabody.'

At the very moment of leaving Boston, jostled at the rail of the ship taking him back to Bsharri, the young Lebanese man could not help thinking about his first muse and wondering if he would ever see her again.

THREE

Back to his Roots

*O*n 30 August 1898, Gibran Khalil Gibran landed ashore in Beirut. In his luggage were seven books, among which were the Gospel and Thomas Bulfinch's *The Age of Fable or Beauties of Mythology*, a book Fred Holland Day had given him. During his voyage, the budding artist discovered the drama of Prometheus, the myth of Orpheus, the Persian poet, Zoroaster, and the philosophy of Pythagoras, as well as Indian mythology.

Gibran went straight to Bsharri and rushed into his father's arms. His father looked defeated, was worried about the future of his family in Boston, and drank like a fish. Friends and relatives rushed to welcome 'the American'. The doctor-poet Selim Daher was moved to see his young disciple again. He advised him to attend Al-Hikma College in Beirut, one of the best schools in the country. It had been founded in 1875 by the Maronite Church and was run by Mgr Yusuf Debs, a prelate who had trained with the Order of the Saint-Sulpice Priests in France. Gibran's father agreed to send his son to study in Beirut and gave him enough money on which to get by.

On 20 October 1898, Gibran enrolled at Al-Hikma College, where he studied until June 1901. Despite the gaps in some of the subjects, such as classical Arabic, the adolescent insisted that he be placed in a class above the one assigned to him and that he not be given any tests for three months. He felt he needed this time to adapt to an educational system that was so new to him. The administration was taken aback by this request, but they were won over by his charming audacity, and they agreed to place him in a higher class.

Father Yusuf Haddad[1] was one of Gibran's teachers. His portrait, hanging in the National Library of Lebanon, shows him as a bearded man with a round forehead, a piercing look, and sporting a black cap. Father Haddad was a teacher unlike any other: using poems and plays, he was able to sway his students towards the arts. Through him, Gibran deepened his knowledge of the Bible and discovered the treasures of the Arabic language by reading Ibn Khaldun,[2] al-Mutanabbi,[3] Ibn Sina and the Sufi poets. He started being able to express his ideas well in his native tongue and began some of his first writings in Arabic. He even drafted the first pages of a book he intended to entitle *So That The Universe Might Be Good*, which ended up being a clumsy version of *The Prophet*. He also learned French and delved avidly into the works of Victor Hugo, Chateaubriand and Rousseau. Father Haddad recollected, 'I could see a beautiful and harmonious whole, and a shape that would not be molded. Gibran was growing quickly. He burst with life and flowed like a spring, and his leaping soul frolicked, now rebelling, now taking strength. "Think a lot. Write little," I would tell him.' Reciprocally, the young man appreciated his teacher immensely and claimed, 'He was the only man who was ever able to teach me anything.'

1. Yusuf Haddad (1865–1949) was born in Ain Kfah (in the District of Jbeil) and took his vows in 1889. He influenced several Lebanese writers, including Amin Takieddine and Michel Zaccour.
2. Arab historian and philosopher (Tunis 1332–Cairo 1406).
3. 'Al-Mutanabbi' literally means 'one who claims prophecy'. It was the epithet of Ahmad Abou al-Taïb (915–65), who was the panegyrist of royalty of his era, but also the author of protest poems flavoured with an epic style.

About his own education, Gibran recollected, 'The first two years in college were hard because of the burden of authority. The college was strict; the teachers here are far freer with their hands than those in America. I didn't believe in their discipline and didn't obey them. I was punished less than the other students were, however, because I made up for it by working hard.' In fact, his teachers were rather indulgent with him because of his status as a returning emigrant. In class, he daydreamed endlessly, drew, and covered his books and copybooks with caricatures of his teachers. The pencil or ink sketches from this period already included symbolism and were a precursor of the visual images to develop later on: women or androgens sitting or lying, suffering or embracing a shape resembling a child.

Gibran's classmates found him strange, what with his long hair, which he refused to cut, and his eccentric attitude. When he told them that he was friends with American editors and that he had drawings on the covers of several books published in New York, they were sceptical. He befriended Ayub Tabet, who in 1943 was appointed by the French authorities as head of the interim government, and Yusuf Huwayyik, the nephew of the Maronite patriarch. Yusuf later became a renowned sculptor whose *Les Pleureuses (The Weepers)*, the tribute to the martyrs, was erected in 1930 in the heart of the Place des Canons in Beirut. Gibran introduced Huwayyik to painting. 'Yusuf was my spiritual child, in a way,' he said about the young boy, whom he later met again in Paris.

Far away, fate finally looked kindly upon Josephine Peabody, who published her first collection of poetry, *The Wayfarers*,[1] in 1898. At her book promotion, she ran into Day. Reminiscing about Gibran, she said, 'The boy was made to be one of the prophets. This is true. His drawings say it clearlier [sic] than anything else could. There is

---

1.   She then went on to publish plays, *Piper*, *Wolf of Gubbio* and *Wings*, among others, as well as a book of tales, *Old Greek Folk Stories*.

no avoiding that young personality. You are filled with recognition and radiant delight. Great spiritual possessions. These you can see in every sketch and a perception, a native-born wisdom that is second sight. I bless the day I saw these things, for there is nothing that so warms one's heart and cheers the thoughts that are growing down in the dark as to meet one of these creatures who are dear to God.' Upon returning home, Posy decided to write to her young friend to thank him for giving her the portrait he had made of her:

> A lovely little surprise came to me, some time ago in the shape of the drawing that you left for me, before you sailed away. At first I found it hard to believe that it really was for me, or that you could have kept me in mind so long ... Very lately I saw and talked with your friend Mr. Day. We spoke of you; and he let me see many more of the drawings that you had left with him. I wish to tell you that they made me feel quite happy for the rest of the day. Why? Because I seemed to understand you through them clearly and I felt sure that you will always have within yourself, a rich happiness to share with other people. You have eyes to see and ears to hear ... I wonder what your country is like, and whether you have some quiet place to grow in ... How many prophets have grown up in solitude, even perhaps tending the sheep (like Apollo in the story, keeping the flocks of King Admetus!) and I wish that all people who *must* be in a lonely country-place for a time, could know how to find the blessing in solitude, like a spring hidden in the desert.

One can imagine Gibran's joy in receiving this missive, Posy's book, and her photograph. Upon reading the missive, he instantly wrote back, trying hard not to make too many English errors in the language he had not yet mastered.

My dear Josephine,
It seems that if I have gained you for a friend after all, 'Have I?'
the hope of that was near the side of its graive Of course I was
so pleased when I saw your picture ... and the little letter from
you to me which will open the door of our friendship. And
as I says that the hope of getting a letter from you was almost
dead ... (I will keep your friendship in the middest of my
heart, and over that many many milles of land and sea I will
allways have a certane love for you and will keep the thought
of you near my heart and will be no sepperation between you
and my mind) ... Days past so readily that I did not seen you
to know you more, untell the love of wisdom caryed me over
that long distance and put me in Byrouth in a college studying
Arabic and French and many things beside.

The letter was naïve and touching. It was signed, 'From your far far
friend, Kahlil Gibran.' As the letter 'P' does not exist in the Arabic
language, he made the mistake of addressing the letter to 'Miss
Beabody'. The young lady was delighted to receive the letter and
copied out her little treasure carefully into her journal for safekeeping.
It seemed that she was not indifferent towards Gibran, but being nine
years her junior, what hope could there be for a relationship between
them?

At the beginning of 1900, with the birth of the new century, Gibran
and his friend Yusuf decided to start a magazine entitled *al-Manara,
al-Haqiqa, al-Nahda*, which translates to *Lighthouse, Truth,
Renaissance*. In it, Gibran published some of his writing illustrated
with his own drawings. This was a memorable experience for him.
He later recollected, 'Yusuf Huwayyik and I published a magazine.
He was the managing director, and I was the editor-in-chief. At first
we printed on poor quality paper. The following year, the school
principal gave us permission to use the school printing facilities.' One

evening, unable to fall asleep, the two friends left their dormitory rooms to go on to the terrace. Yusuf reminisces, 'Gibran initiated me to the firmament, the celestial bodies, and the boundless universe. He told me that Earth was nothing but a speck of dust in the crater of an immense volcano and that people who thought they knew God actually knew absolutely nothing. Like an infinite ladder, man's feet are on the ground and his head is in the sky.'

In July, Gibran went back to Bsharri for the summer. His father's irascible mood had not improved. He frequently hurt him, berated his 'frenzy', and could not understand his wanting to dedicate himself to painting or literature. Still beaten by his brush with the police, he hoped Gibran would become a lawyer. The young man wearied of his father's never-ending tirades, so he left home and went to live in the basement of a country house belonging to a notable of the market town, Raji Daher, or at his Aunt Leila's. He spent his days reading near the entrance of Mar Sarkis; at night he often slept outdoors.

Gibran took advantage of the summer lull to get in touch with Dr Selim Daher again. The latter recited poems to him, told him stories, which Gibran copied into his copybooks, and read him the 'Song of Songs' and other passages from the Bible. Thanks to him, Gibran was introduced to Hala, the eldest daughter of the eminent Tannus Hanna Daher, who fell under his spell. But Iskandar, the brother of the young girl, watched him like a hawk. He made it clear to the 'stranger' that the relationship could go nowhere; there was too wide a gap in the status of the two families. Besides, Hala was two years older than Gibran. In this part of Lebanon, it was unwise to mess about with love, so Gibran did not pursue the matter any further.

Several months later, Gibran, now eighteen, met Sultana Tabet, the sister of Ayub, his old classmate. She was twenty-two and had just lost her husband. By Gibran's own admission, 'She was beautiful, talented, and loved poetry.' His portrait of her, which depicts her big bright eyes, long hair, sensual lips, and fine chin, seems to confirm this impression. For four months, they saw each other, exchanging books and sharing their comments on them.

> I was eighteen years old when love opened my eyes with its magical rays and touched my spirit for the first time with its fiery fingers ... What man does not remember the first girl, who, through her sweetness and innocence, transformed the indolence of his youth into a formidable awakening, poignant and ravaging? ... Every young man remembers his first love and tries to recapture that strange hour, the memory of which changes his deepest feeling and makes him so happy in spite of all of the bitterness of its mystery. Who would not be consumed by nostalgia at the memory of this strange moment? ... During that period, I was vacillating between the influences of nature and inspired interpretation of books and the Scriptures when Salma's lips spoke the words of love into the ear of my soul,

In this extract from *Broken Wings*, Salma Karamé, the heroine, resembles Sultana Tabet. But this love was short-lived. Sultana's sudden death filled Gibran with incredibly profound sadness. People sent him objects that had belonged to her: a silk handkerchief, some jewels and a parcel of seventeen letters. These were love letters that the young woman had written without ever having dared send to him. 'No one could imagine the pain that I felt. Why hadn't she sent them to me earlier?' he wrote.

At school, Gibran the student was making progress. In July 1901, he won a merit award for one of his poems. 'I tried very hard to win the poetry contest. It is a major event in the life of a student. For Al-Hikma College, excellence was determined by talent in poetry. I had high hopes to win the prize.' On the eve of results, he had seen Christ in a dream. Was that a premonition? When he awoke, he found he had won first prize.

During this time, back in the USA, Fred Holland Day, absorbed with photography, decided to shut down his publishing house, which had published almost a hundred titles but which was never very lucrative, and decided to fulfil one of his dreams, a trip to the East. Did he meet up with Gibran during his voyage? There does not seem to be any proof that he did, but there are a few slight indications suggesting that possibility. We do know that Day went to Algeria. There is a letter from Gibran, dated 5 April 1901, in which the young man tells his father that he intends to go on a tour to Syria and Palestine, as well as the land of the Nile, in the company of an American family. In another letter to May Ziadeh, he wrote, 'When I was in Egypt, twice a week I would spend long hours sitting on the golden sand, my eyes riveted towards the pyramids and the sphinx. I was eighteen at the time. My soul trembled in face of the architectural phenomena like grass rustles in a storm.' But these shreds of evidence are by no means conclusive.

At the end of this trip, Gibran started to prepare his return to the United States; his apprenticeship was over, and he missed his family. He was informed that his sister Sultana was sick. He was confused; could this be true? Had she made up this piece of news so that he would return to her straightaway? Without further ado, Gibran took to the sea in April 1902. On leaving Lebanon he gave his cousin, Boulos Bitar Kayrouz, the seven books he had brought back with him from Boston, along with notes and some sketches of a woman, of John the Baptist, and of a sunset, hoping to reclaim them one day. But, in his heart of hearts, he knew he would never return: 'The chants of Lebanon will only ever reach my ears in a dream.'

FOUR

Tragic Events

1902: On his way back to the States, Gibran stopped in Paris, but bad news awaited him there. He was devastated to learn that Sultana, only fourteen years old, had died on 4 April. Not only was she too young to die, she was also the sibling, according to Day, who resembled Gibran the most – both physically and in character. He could neither fathom nor accept what had happened. According to Mariana, his other sister, two years previously one ganglion on each side of Sultana's neck had started to grow. The doctor prescribed medication but confessed to Boutros that there was not much hope because she would not be able to undergo surgery. A year later, in September 1901, she contracted a rapidly deteriorating case of consumption. Then one day a few months later, Sultana showed Mariana her legs swollen all the way up to the knees and cried out bitterly to her sister, 'Now I'll never be able to get up again.' As a matter of fact, she was unable to walk from that day onwards. She often sighed that she missed Gibran and her father and expressed her longing to see them, claiming that if she could, if only for an instant, she would then be able to die in peace.

Arriving in Boston on 13 April, Gibran was greeted by his family, who were crushed by the loss of the young Sultana and still in tears. With a twisted sense of propriety, he avoided talking about his deceased sister, thinking that if he did, he would only be driving the knife further into the family wound. He baffled them by not mentioning her but respected Lebanese mourning traditions by getting a haircut and wearing black.

Several days later, the Gibrans left 9 Oliver Place to settle in 7 Tyler Street, near Our Lady of the Cedars, the Maronite church. The parish priest, Mgr Istiphan Douaihy, lived in the same building, and he often dropped in on his neighbours to console them or discuss religion with Gibran. It was around this time that the young man asked his mother for advice about the book he had drafted in Lebanon, *So That The Universe Might Be Good,* the embryo of his later book, *The Prophet*. She wisely told him, 'Give it time to ferment.' Although she never doubted her son's capabilities, Kamila did not think the time was yet ripe; she believed his ideas were still incipient and that he needed to develop them. Gibran accepted her advice, and he let the book germinate in his spirit for the next twenty years.

And Josephine? Apparently, mourning for Sultana had taken Gibran's mind off her for a while, but on 6 November he finally wrote to her that he was back. During the four years he was away, she had kept busy. She had published two books and a play, and after teaching at Wellesley College, she spent a summer in England. Receiving the letter from her admirer, Josephine answered him the next day, inviting him to a reception on Sunday, 16 November. He didn't think twice about accepting, and their reunion was warm. Without really being in love with the young man, Posy was flattered to be his muse. 'If I see him much of him, he will turn me into a Buddha!' she wrote in her diary. In fact, she was quite fascinated by the ideas and the artwork of this young man, who was so different from everybody else. 'And at present he is drawing and writing Arabic poems and essays. As for the drawings, we shall see them. If they have developed in any proportion at all to the early ones, he will shake up the world ... The knowledge of this beautiful heart of a young prophet has been a comfort to me all these years.' The word *prophet* was premonitory, for Josephine was undoubtedly one of the first to have perceived the spirituality inherent in the work of this mystic, this genius that her sister Marion considered an angel.

Posy and Gibran began to spend more time together. They wrote frequently, went to concerts, and attended a performance of Wagner's *Percival*. He gave her an assortment of presents: a *nay* and a new portrait in pastels signed eloquently as if it were a proposition, 'Beware, o Soul, as love is talking to you, so you must listen. Unlock your heart and welcome love, you will be extolled.' To him, she was the dear friend, the beloved, the sweet love. He signed all his letters to her with his initials GKG inscribed in arabesque lettering. In her diary, that is how Posy referred to him. He was her soulmate and a creature of genius, and in an attempt to become his godmother, she managed to get his drawings exhibited at Wellesley College in May 1903. She was the source of his inspiration, yet there was something presumptuous, bordering on the arrogant, in her attitude, which was rather disquieting. Josephine – whom Gibran found vain about her beauty – was convinced that she was nurturing the talent of the young artist and that she had become indispensable to his equilibrium and his creativity. She once wrote that every time she stretched out her hands filled with hope, he drew forth ideas, happiness and fulfilment and that listening to him thanking her, she would watch him leave with freedom and glory in his heart. And to top it off, she added, 'All I can do is to continue existing for him.' She considered her friend as 'a wounded lamb of the flock of our Lord that I have the good fortune to nourish in a way.' As if her role of muse was not enough, Posy set herself up as his saviour and his Pygmalion.

Each of them was going through a rough patch, and their bond of friendship became stronger during these times of adversity. 'The sorrowful spirit finds rest when united with a similar one,' wrote Gibran. 'Hearts that are united through the medium of sorrow will not be separated by the glory of happiness.' For Josephine, it was all about friendship. Gibran, on the other hand, deified the young woman so much that she became the embodiment or personification of femininity, the prelude to his feminine superior being called 'She'. In this context, a physical relationship between them was highly unlikely. He wrote, 'and my love does not give birth to desire, does not harbor any selfish thoughts. It is the weak in spirit who give in to the desires of the flesh: they cannot love.'

Their closeness, however, was short-lived. In October 1903, something must have happened to upset the applecart. Posy reproached Gibran for 'your infuriating suggestion more or less'. What was that about? Could it have been a declaration of love? A marriage proposal? Something else? She was so angry with him that she tore up all the letters he had sent her after August. Why did she destroy those but keep the previous ones? Undoubtedly, Gibran must have changed his attitude towards her at that point. Perhaps in August he had started writing things that she would have preferred to forget ... As of May, the letters of Gibran had become bolder. 'I have just said good morning to the rose which you gave me last night and I kissed its lips; you kissed them too.' Had the poet continued in the same vein?

They did not stop writing to each other, although the tone of their letters changed, and they did continue seeing each other from time to time. He spent Christmas Eve and his twenty-second birthday with her. Soon enough, though, Gibran and Posy finally realised that their relationship was based on a misunderstanding. He loved her; she merely loved that he loved her, and gradually, they grew apart. As a breaking-up present, he gave her an antique silver ring, 200 years old, that his maternal grandfather, Father Istiphan, had taken off the hand of a statue of the Virgin Mary to give him on his baptism. Gibran must have adored Posy to part with such a treasure! He drew her portrait and wrote two lines in English, very revealing of his feelings for her. 'I loved you with confidence – now I love you with fear – I love you more than I ever did but I am afraid of you.' Overwhelmed by her financial woes, the young woman threw herself into the arms of an Englishman, Lionel Marks, a Harvard professor. Gibran did not look favourably on this rival, who had an abundance of diplomas and a promising future. He became self-conscious of his own weakness and naïveté. But the dice had been rolled. In 1906, Posy married her suitor, and although Gibran was invited to the wedding, he declined to attend.

Meanwhile, fate dealt another cruel blow to the Gibran family. In Boston – more precisely in the South End of Boston – tuberculosis was taking its terrible toll. Boutros, constantly in touch with customers, was exposed to the disease and started coughing. The doctor who examined him recommended that he return to Lebanon to get away from the polluted air of the infected city. So as not to have to travel too far away from the family and still be able to sell his merchandise, Boutros preferred to settle in Cuba. For all the precautions he took, it was to no avail; he was wasting away and getting thinner by the day.

As if that were not enough, on 15 December 1902, Kamila was hospitalised for a tumour she had developed. Mariana, the only one still able to work and support the family, sat at her bedside at Massachusetts General Hospital. 'My mother had an operation. As she was coming out of surgery, the surgeon confided to a family friend that my mother had cancer. I asked Gibran to tell me what "cancer" was in Arabic. Bit by bit, he explained, and our tears flowed. Shortly afterwards, he was able to bring her home, thus allowing her to live her last days peacefully among us.' One week after Kamila was discharged from the hospital, Boutros returned from Cuba. He had lost so much weight that his own sister did not even recognise him. Boutros slept in one room, Kamila in another. Mariana slept on a mattress in the hallway separating the two rooms. Deeply shattered, Gibran wrote (in Arabic), rebelling against the indifference of destiny, which spared nothing or no one.

> I write strange thoughts, ideas passing like flocks of birds. What is my life worth? Who would want it? ... What good are all these great hopes, a lot of books and strange drawings? What use is this learning that I have acquired? What more is this earth with its gaping mouth and bared chest demanding?

As the condition of the two patients worsened, Mariana became desperate. How could she attend to their needs and alleviate their final pain and suffering, as it was certainly their last? No one harboured any illusions about their recovery or survival. She continued to work to make enough money for the medication. Day, whom Gibran affectionately called 'my dear older brother', sent them food, but that was not enough. That is when Gibran was spurred into action. Putting aside his prejudices about commerce and businessmen, he decided to take over care of the shop. On 7 March, Josephine wrote about this in her diary.

> Gibran was here yesterday and most unhappy. But he had done a very fine thing – entirely against his strongest inclinations – to save the business honor of his brother who is hopelessly ill. He thought it would be dishonorable – or at least 'very easy' to claim bankruptcy, so he made up his mind to revive the business, if he could, till the creditors could at least get their money back; and he has persuaded the chief creditor to be his partner. Behold Gibran a businessman for the time – fast bound in misery and iron? I know with all my heart,

the anguish it will be to him; and yet I am filled with pride
that my Genius was strong enough to grasp the situation that
hurts him most and grasp it strongly. Win out of it – he must
and then soon ...

On Thursday, 12 March 1903, Boutros, only twenty-six years old,
passed away. Gibran was grief-stricken and wrote to Day to tell him
the news. 'The dear brother went home, at 3 o'clock in the morning,
leaving us in the depth of sorrow and broken hearted. I must console
my ailing mother. Marianna and I can see the darkness of the future.'
The next day Josephine wrote in her journal, 'My genius has lost his
brother; I suppose the poor mother can hardly live longer now. And
what do to for him I am helpless to know – There is nothing in the
world to do; I can only be.' Josephine did not realise how true her
prediction would turn out to be. On 28 June 1903, Mariana helplessly
witnessed Kamila taking her last breath. Five minutes after her death,
at six PM, Gibran, who had gone to open the shop, came home. Upon
seeing his mother dead, he fainted and started bleeding from his nose
and mouth. When he came to, he bent over to gaze at Kamila's face.
'In all my life, I never saw anything as divine as the expression of glory
that haloed over her ... The melody reposed in silence at the bottom
of my mother's heart will forever be sung on the lips of her child.' He
remained faithful to her memory for the rest of his days.

Within fifteen months, tragedy had struck three times. Gibran
confessed, 'Kamila was not only my mother, she was a friend. My
life is now shrouded.' On 29 June, he wrote to Day, 'My mother will
not suffer any longer, but we poor children are suffering and longing
for her.' Death having devastated his family, Khalil, his father, sank
into despair. He left his house to his creditors and went to live in the
rotting basement of Raji Daher, adding to the triple tragedy a fourth:
his own.

As his mother had invested the money of several of her Syrian friends, Gibran felt obligated to pay them back. He ended up selling his brother's business to pay back all the debts and alleviate himself of the burden, but he knew he had to pull out of the business because it was consuming his life. Now free, he could think about resuming his artistic career. Who could he turn to other than Fred Holland Day?

FIVE

Beginnings

Nicknamed 'the Athens of America', Boston was, at the dawn of the twentieth century, an important intellectual centre to which promising or established artists gravitated. A number of them, sickened by the poor taste stemming from the industrial economy, wanted to step out of the bulwark of materialism. They searched for new artistic venues and explored not only mythology and Oriental civilisations but also occult sciences and spiritualism in the hopes that spirituality would nurture their inspiration and provide them with equilibrium. Gibran immersed himself in this Bostonian society, where mystic movements like New Thought, the Theosophical Society and Christian Science abounded. Swedenborg, Phineas Quimby, and Warren Felt Evans were far removed from the institutionalised religions and believed in the uniqueness of existence, the divine essence of human beings, and reincarnation. The most striking of these doctrines was undoubtedly theosophy. It was founded in 1875 by Helena Petrovna Blavatsky, a Russian aristocrat who had explored the wisdom of India, Tibet and the Druzes (whom she visited in Syria and Lebanon in 1865 and 1872). She inspired the rebirth of Buddhism and Hinduism, contributed to making knowledge of Oriental thought in the West more widespread, and rekindled an interest in metempsychosis. In contact with the entourage of Fred Holland Day, who was not himself a member of the Theosophical Society,[1] and later Charlotte Teller, Gibran discovered the ideas propounded by this movement. He soon realised that the Oriental spiritualism within him could find a fertile ground in his current environment starved of mysticism.

On 6 January 1904, Fred Holland Day suggested that Gibran exhibit his paintings that spring at Harcourt Studios, a building comprising about forty studios belonging to poor painters and photographers in town, including himself. The young artist gladly accepted although he realised how difficult it would be to turn out new paintings or drawings as well as touch up the existing ones with only four months in which to do so. Influenced by the mythology of William Blake, he completed several drawings containing strong symbolism. In March, exhausted by relentless work and the unhealthy climate of Boston, he fell ill. His sister and his friends were very worried about him and wondered if he had been infected and contracted tuberculosis. Would he survive? Luckily, he pulled through.

His exhibition at Harcourt Studios ran from 30 April to 10 May. It drew many spectators but few buyers. In the *Evening Transcript* a critic analysed Gibran's work perfectly and summarised his style and method of work. 'The ponderous beauty and nobility of certain of his pictorial fancies are wonderful; and the tragic import of other conceptions is dreadful. All told, his drawings make a profound impression, and, considering his age, the qualities shown in them are extraordinary for originality and depth of symbolic significance ... All

---

1. 'Day never followed the path of Theosophy or Christian Science, two radical new religious cults of the time which had a devoted following in Boston,' wrote Anne E. Havinga in 'Setting the Time of Day in Boston' (in Pam Roberts, *Fred Holland Day*, Van Gogh Museum, Amsterdam 2001).

these drawings are, as their titles imply, spiritual allegories of the most solemn character and import. The earnest desire to give expression to metaphysical ideas has triumphantly prevailed over technical limitations to the extent that the imagination is greatly stirred by the abstract or moral beauty of the thought ... which express the purest aspirations of the most subtle shades of moral moods.'

It was during the course of this exhibition that Gibran met Mary Haskell, who was later to play a significant role in his life and become his 'guardian angel'. Originally from an affluent family in Columbia, South Carolina, she was the daughter of an ex-officer of the Confederate Army who became vice president of Columbia Bank. Mary settled in New England to pursue her studies at Wellesley College. Attracted by the intellectual atmosphere of Boston, she decided to stay there and set up the Haskell School for Girls on 314 Marlborough Street. She was constantly helping young, struggling artists and enthusiastically championed social and political causes. This hardened feminist, keen on swimming and hiking, loved all life's pleasures; so was it to free herself from the grip of her conservative family that she settled in Boston? It would seem likely, as her love life was complicated and disorganised, and her love or sexual relations often seemed ambivalent.

Invited by Lionel Marks, Posy's future husband, Mary arrived at Harcourt Studios on Tuesday, 10 May, the last day of the exhibition. Gibran noticed the young woman, dressed in black and wearing a silver belt, who seemed to be intrigued by one of his drawings. She was ten years his senior. Where did Gibran's attraction to older women stem from? Was it his search for a mother figure? Or was it, simply, his maturity that put him within their reach? Mary was not particularly beautiful. She had an athletic build, a long face, thick eyebrows and a complexion tanned by excursions in the Californian mountains. Her light brown hair was not well groomed, but her face shone and her blue eyes sparkled. Taking his courage in both hands, Gibran accosted her as she was lingering over a pencil drawing. Thus began their first real conversation, of which this is not an exact transcription but conveys the spirit of their dialogue:

'Would you like me to interpret these pictures for you?'

'With pleasure. I'm afraid I need this art explained to me as it is not the kind one is used to seeing. It is true that I love art, but I myself am not an artist. Are you?'

'Yes, I am honoured to be one.'

'Do you know this artist?'

'I am he.'

Mary stared at him wide-eyed and scrutinised the young, short, and dark painter facing her. 'You? Surely you must have studied art in Paris.'

'No, actually, I am self-taught – with the assistance of some Bostonian artists.'

'So young, and so talented! Tell me, why are all the bodies in your paintings nudes?'

'Because the truth is naked. And the naked body is the closest and most beautiful symbol of life.'

'And why all these symbols of death and suffering?'

'Because death and pain have always been a part of my life. In a span of two years, I lost my sister, my brother and my mother. Each one of them held a special place in my heart.'

'I share your pain. And the tears of my heart understand the tear in your eye. Like you, I have just lost my mother. So we have two things in common: art and pain.'

'The link of pain is stronger than the bond of joy or ties of the blood.'

Mary thanked the artist, asked him how the exhibition had gone, and invited him to visit the school she had founded and of which she was principal.

Gibran would never forget this. He later told Mary that he knew that people at the exhibition liked to get him talking, because he was an oddity for them. It was like people watching a monkey. She, on the other hand, was different. She seemed to be genuinely interested in listening to what he had to say, to incite him to talk by reaching into his own depths. He was won over.

Four days later, Gibran was invited to tea at the Haskell School. When Mary suggested that he exhibit his work there for two weeks, he jumped at the chance. By the end of that exhibition, they had started seeing each other frequently.

After a short stay at Day's Five Islands summer home on the beach, Gibran went back to Boston. He was determined to find more lucrative work than being a painter. He was tormented by scruples. His sister, Mariana, was killing herself working at the sewing workshop to cover their living expenses. He found out that a young Lebanese immigrant named Amin Gorayeb had just established an Arabic newspaper, *al-Mohajer* ('The Emigrant'), in New York. Gibran invited Gorayeb to his home and showed him his drawings and the laudatory critiques of his work as well as his notebook sprinkled with prose poems in Arabic. Gorayeb immediately agreed to hire his compatriot as a writer for two dollars a week. Several months later, Gibran's first article, 'Vision', a lyrical text which gave voice to 'the heart of man, captive of materialism and victim of the laws of mortals', was published.

On 12 November 1904, disaster struck: Harcourt Studios burnt down. A ravaging fire destroyed the forty studios and reduced to ashes the materials and photos of Fred Holland Day, 2,000 negatives in total, as well as the drawings that Gibran had left in Day's safekeeping. For Day, it was the destruction of eighteen years of work. For Gibran, it was another notch in the string of tragedies that had started two years earlier.

Disillusioned, to Josephine's attempt at consolation he could only reply, 'The important thing is to know that we are still alive.' Mary Haskell also sent him a letter of sympathy to lift his spirits, the first of what would become a twenty-three-year correspondence of 625 revealing letters, sometimes too lyrical. To her he responded, 'My dear Miss Haskell, it is the sympathy of friends that makes grief a sweet sorrow.'

In *al-Mohajer*, as if to exorcise the bad luck that had befallen him, he published a remarkable poem, eloquently entitled 'Letters of Fire'.

> *Shall death destroy that which we build*
> *And the winds scatter our words,*
> *And darkness hide our deeds?*
> *Is this then life? ...*
> *... Shall man be even as the foam*
> *That sits an instant on the ocean's face*
> *And is taken by the passing breeze –*
> *And is no more?*
> *No, in truth, for the verity of life is life;*
> *Life whose birth is not in the womb*
> *Nor its end in death ...*
> *... Yonder in the hereafter*
> *We shall see the beating of our hearts*
> *And comprehend the meaning of our godlike state,*
> *That in this day we hold as naught*
> *Because despair is ever at our heels ...*
> *... The afflictions that we bear*
> *Shall be to us a crown of honor.*

Still suffering from the shock of the fire, Gibran wrote more than he drew. 'I do not know what to do with my colored pencils at present; perhaps they will be kept in the chest of forgetfulness,' he confided to Mary. From then onwards, he held a regular column, 'Thoughts' (later 'A Tear and a Smile'), in Gorayeb's newspaper. He began his first texts writing about love, beauty, youth, and wisdom. In 1905 the *al-Mohajer*

printers of 21 Washington Street in New York published his first
a short essay in Arabic entitled *Music*, which in a stylised manner
represents music as if it is a loved one, a source of memories and feelings
that can transport the human soul beyond the material world.

'Music is the language of spirits. Its melody is like the frolicsome
breeze that makes the strings quiver with love. When the gentle fingers
of Music knock at the door of our feelings, they awaken memories
that have long lain hidden in the depths of the Past.'

It was at about this time that the journalist Naseeb Arida suggested
interviewing Gibran using a questionnaire inspired by Proust.[1] The
young artist complied without hesitation:

'What do you find to be the most beautiful thing in nature?'
  'The mountain,' he replied, undoubtedly thinking of Bsharri.
  'And what is your favorite season?'
  'Autumn.'
  'Which smell do you like best?'
  'The kindling of fire.'
  'What is your favorite name?'
  'Salma.'
  'Which sculptures do you like?'
  'Those of Michelangelo.'[2]
  'Who are your favorite poets?'
  'Shakespeare, al-Mutanabbi, Majnoun Layla,[3] Abu Nuwas[4] ... they
were all madmen.'

---

1. This questionnaire is cited by Jamil Jabre in *Gibran dans son époque et dans son œuvre littéraire et artistique*, Naufal, 1983, p. 54.

2. On 3 September 1923 Gibran sent May Ziadeh a postcard illustrating one of Michelangelo's sculptures in which he extols the genius of the artist.

3. 'Majnoun Layla' lived in the eighth century. He spent his life writing and dedicating his work to the woman for whom his love led him to the brink of insanity.

4. Al-Hassan Ibn Hani (around 762–813 AD) celebrates wine and love in his work.

'And your favorite prose authors?'

'Ibn Khaldun for this thinking, Nietzsche for his imagination, and Tourgueniev for his images.'

'What about your fictional heroes?'

'Hamlet, Brutus,[1] Francesca da Rimini.'[2]

'Which period of history would you have liked to live in?'

'The present, as it comprises all the past.'

'Which country would you like to live in?'

'Lebanon.'

'What character trait do you admire most in men?'

'Loyalty.'

'And in women?'

'Purity.'

'If you were not Gibran Khalil Gibran, who would you want to be?'

'Gibran Khalil Gibran.'

'According to you, what are the gentlest words?'

'Love, Nature, God.'

'What is your aim in life?'

'To work, work, and work.'

'Who is the historical figure you admire most?'

'Mohammed.'

'And your favorite heroine?'

'Xenobia and Joan of Arc.'

'Which books do you like reading best?'

'*The Book of Job*, *Macbeth*, and *King Lear*.'

This was a revealing interview. At twenty-three, Gibran admitted to

---

1. Probably Shakespeare's Brutus.
2. Heroine of the fifth cantos of 'Hell' in *The Divine Comedy* of Dante. She is the daughter of a lord of Ravenne, and she is married off to Gianciotto Malatesta, son of the tyrant Rimini. She is caught with her lover, and they are both killed.

being influenced by Michelangelo, Shakespeare, Nietzsche and the *Book of Job*. He was firmly determined to find and be himself and to focus on his work. He had a fascination with 'madmen' and as additional proof to his open-mindedness, he paid homage to both Mohammed and Joan of Arc. He clearly affirmed his attachment to his native country. As for his answers related to Salma and Francesca da Rimini, they are precursors to his works *Broken Wings* and *Spirits Rebellious,* in which the story entitled 'The Bridal Couch' echoes Francesca's tragedy in Dante's work. It cannot be reiterated enough that from a tender young age, be it in his writing or his drawing, Gibran plotted out his career with precision.

In the autumn of 1906, Gibran published *The Nymphs of the Valley*, an anthology of three allegorical stories in Arabic. 'Dust of the Ages and the Eternal Fire' tells the story of a Phoenician priest who loses his fiancée and who, 2,000 years later, is reincarnated as a shepherd and rediscovers her in a peasant girl. 'Martha' is the story of an orphan girl who is seduced and then abandoned by a rich city-dweller. Gibran takes the opportunity to criticise social inequality and to castigate man's exploitation of women. 'Yuhanna the Mad' tells of the wrangles of a shepherd with the monks in a monastery and condemns despotism and the rapacity of the clergy in times past. 'Come again, Oh living Jesus,' declared Yuhanna the Mad, 'and drive the vendors of Thy faith away from Thy sacred temple, for they have turned it into a dark cave where vipers of hypocrisy and falsehood crawl and abound.' The work, coloured with romanticism, exposes themes dear to the author's heart: the greatness of Christ contrasted with the pettiness of the clergy; madness as a source of truth and liberty; and metempsychosis:

I am going, my beloved, to the meadows of the spirits, but I shall return to this world. Astarte brings back to this life the souls of lovers who have gone into the infinite before they have tasted the delights of love and the joys of youth.

As soon as it was published, the work aroused suspicion in Arabic countries. Gibran was aware of this and wrote to his cousin, Nakhli:

> In Syria, people label me impious, and in Egypt men of letters denigrate me by claiming, 'He is the enemy of just laws, of family ties, and of ancestral traditions.' These people are telling the truth. I know that my soul abhors man-made laws, and I abhor traditions that bind future generations. This hatred is the fruit of my love for the sacred and spiritual kindness which should be the source for every law upon the earth, for kindness is the shadow of God in man ... I know that there is a great power in the depth of my heart that wants to reveal itself, and it will manifest itself in due time if it is the will of Heaven.

These were the premonitory words of an artist who, like a prophet, knew he had a mission to accomplish.

SIX

The City of Light

*G*ibran celebrated his twenty-fourth birthday on 6 January 1907, at Mary Haskell's school, where he had been invited for tea. He arrived with a signed copy of his latest book and, as if on first contact with his 'patron of art', the creative spirit within him broke free. He retreated to a corner of the room and made two sketches. Several months later, he granted her request to do a self-portrait using a female face as the background. He dated the painting 1908, dedicated it to MEH (Mary Elizabeth Haskell), and signed it with a peculiar monogram of her initials.

It was around this same time that Gibran started seeing a pianist, Gertrude Barrie, on the sly. She then became his mistress, and they carried on at the young woman's studio, on the second floor of a building at 552 Tremont Street. Their relationship lasted for several years without ever having left a trace on any of his writings.

At the start of 1908, Mary invited Gibran, along with two of her friends, to dinner. The first was Charlotte Teller, a divorced journalist. At thirty-two, this extrovert socialised with theosophists and wanted to become a successful writer. Appleton had just published her novel,

The Cage. She nursed a real passion for Mary, as evidenced by what she once wrote to her, 'No one loves me as you do, nor do I love anyone as I love you.' The second friend was a Frenchwoman, Emilie Michel, who was only twenty, and whom Mary had recruited on a trip to Europe and brought back to Boston to teach French at the Haskell School. Keen on theatre, the young girl dreamed of going on the stage and taking Broadway by storm.

There was a definite chemistry among the three guests, and that evening Gibran, who found Charlotte 'strangely beautiful', sketched her portrait. He also grasped the opportunity to expound his theories on art and God to the young ladies. 'Most religions speak of God in the masculine gender. To me He is as much a mother as He is a Father. He is both the father and the mother in one; and Woman is the God-Mother. The God-Father may be reached through the mind or the imagination. But the God-Mother can be reached through the heart only – through love.'

All evening long, Mary gazed at Gibran, at his long, silky eyelashes and his eyes like 'stars reflected in a deep water'. She admired his face, which 'changed like the shades of leaves, at every thought, with every feeling', and 'his simple, ephemeral beauty, which no image could do justice to'. This inspired man was different from all the others; he was made of the stuff of prophets. She knew she had to take his career into her hands.

Shortly afterwards, Mary invited Gibran to her school to show the students a drawing lesson in action, at which time he took the opportunity to draw a portrait of Emilie Michel. Mary followed this up by an invitation into her home. They drank coffee, smoked cigarettes and talked about the future. Gibran confessed that he did not feel he was making progress any more and that he needed to move forward. She suggested sending him to Paris for a year, at her own expense, so that he could better himself. Gibran was flabbergasted; he knew Mary was caring, but he had no idea she would be so generous, so devoted to his well-being. Paris! He had always dreamed of visiting the City of Light. In a letter to Jamil Malouf, a young Lebanese poet, he wrote,

> I have heard that you are going to return to Paris to live there. I, too, would like to go there. Is it possible that we both could meet in the City of Arts? Will we meet in the Heart of the World to visit the Opéra and the Comédie Française, and talk about the plays of Racine, Corneille, Molière, Hugo, and Sardou? Will we meet there and walk together to where the Bastille was erected and then return to our quarters feeling the gentle spirit of Rousseau and Voltaire and write about Liberty and Tyranny and destroy every Bastille that stands in every city in the East? Will we go to the Louvre and stand before the paintings of Raphael, Da Vinci, and Corot, and write about Beauty and Love and their influence on the hearts of men?

The evening of 12 February, Gibran, referring undoubtedly to Haskell, wrote to Amin Gorayeb, 'The she-angel I found in Boston is ushering me towards a splendid future and paving a path of intellectual and financial success for me. God willing, this is the beginning of a new chapter in the story of my life.' On 28 March, he wrote to his editor, who was in Lebanon at the time, that he was leaving Boston, the noisy, boisterous city, for Paris. 'I am in these days like a man observing Lent and awaiting the coming of the dawn and the feast. My imminent trip to Paris causes my dreams to hover around the great achievements I hope will be mine during my year in the City of Knowledge and Arts … I am sure that you will pass through Paris on your way back to the United States. In Paris we shall meet and be merry.'

Before Gibran's departure, *al-Mohajer* published his third book in Arabic, *Spirits Rebellious*. He used four realistic stories set in

Lebanon to express his revolt against the oppression of feudalists, the clergy and the courts. He forcefully denounced the subjection of the Eastern world to old-fashioned traditions. Although blurred by the forcefulness of his revolutionary ideas, the inherent spirituality that was to characterise his future work is not totally obscured:

> The true light is the one that shines from within; it reveals the secrets of the heart to the soul, making it happy and contented with life ... God has given you a spirit with wings on which to soar into the spacious firmament of Love and Freedom. Is it not pitiful then that you cut your wings with your own hands and suffer your soul to crawl like an insect upon the earth?

The first story, 'Warda al Hani', is a condemnation of arranged marriages. 'The Cry of the Graves' records three appeals presented by people unjustly condemned to death: a young man, who in legitimate self-defence kills an officer, a wrongfully accused adulteress and an old servant who had stolen wheat for survival. 'The Bridal Couch' tells the true story of a young woman who slays herself and her beloved on the night of her wedding to a man she never loved. 'Khalil the Heretic' is the story of a novice who is kicked out of the monastery and is taken in by a woman and her daughter. He is slandered and taken to court. But, against all odds, the court decides in his favour. He ridicules the judges and instigates the revolt of the villagers. In a poem on Liberty, Gibran affirms:

> *In order to secure their power and to rest at heart's ease, they*
> *Have armed the Durzi to fight the Arab;*
> *Have instigated the Shi'i against the Sunni;*
> *Have incited the Kurd to slaughter the Bedouin;*
> *Have encouraged the Mohammadan to fight the Christian –*
> *How long is a brother to fight his brother on the breast of the*
> *mother?*

... How long are the Cross and the Crescent to remain apart before
  the eyes of God?
Listen to us, O Liberty, and harken unto us ...
... Disperse with your resolve these dark clouds;
Descend as a thunderbolt,
Destroy like a catapult
The props of those thrones erected on bones and skulls,
Plated with the gold of taxes and bribery
And soaked in blood and tears.

Several years later, in a letter to Mary, he declared, 'You know I am called the Grave-Digger now, very often. Some think I'm bitter and destructive – but you can't build without tearing down ... The gentle touch does not wake people.' *Spirits Rebellious* starts with this precept. It is a work marked with such commitment and romanticism one is tempted to compare it to the work of Victor Hugo. Its violent touches and vehement tone are reminiscent of *Les Châtiments*. The book certainly made waves in Syria and Egypt. According to certain sources, the Ottoman authorities even burned the book, along with other works they considered 'subversive', in a public square in Beirut.

Gibran was eager to send Mary *Spirits Rebellious* with the following dedication, 'To the spirit that did embrace my spirit. To the heart that did pour out its secrets into my heart. To the hand that did kindle the flame of my love.' On 25 March, he wrote her a letter in which he claims to have mingled with Christ.

My soul is intoxicated today. For last night I dreamt of Him who gave the Kingdom of heaven to man. O if I could only describe Him to you: if I could only tell you of the sad joy in His eyes, the bitter sweetness of His lips, the beauty of His large hands, the rough woolen garment, and the bare feet – so delicately veiled with white dust. And it was all so natural and clear. The mist that makes other dreams so dim was not there. I sat near Him and talked to Him as if I had always lived with

Him. I do not remember His words – and yet I feel them now as one feels in the morning the impression of the music he heard the night before ... The hunger of my heart today is greater and deeper than all days. I am intoxicated with hunger. My soul is thirsty for that which is lofty and great and beautiful. And yet I cannot write nor draw nor read. I can only sit alone in silence and contemplate the Unseen.

When did Gibran's fascination with Jesus start? Was it in his childhood, lived out in a pious milieu devoted to the Virgin Mary and to Christ, whose Passion they shared on Good Friday to such an extent that they went so far as to act it out? Or was it because he felt a strong identification with the ideas of a Superior Being who sided with the downtrodden and preached tolerance and love? Did he really see Him in a dream, or was he imagining visions of ecstasy to enhance his image of the 'Oriental prophet' vis-à-vis his friends? One thing is for certain: all his life, Gibran held a boundless admiration for the 'Son of Man'.

Mary and Gibran met regularly, but although she herself admitted that her protégé consumed more and more of her thoughts and dreams, their relationship had not yet overstepped the boundaries of friendship. On the other hand, there was chemistry between him and the young French teacher, Emilie Michel, nicknamed Micheline by Mary because she felt the melodic nickname suited her charm. Micheline had the profile of a tragic actress, with her long hair thrown back, her long neck, her rather pronounced nose, and her large, expressive eyes with well-defined eyebrows. The young girl enjoyed the company of the artist. She read him poems in French and had no qualms posing nude for him. Gradually, they become fonder of each other. Realising that 'this boy can be easily hurt', she made an effort not to offend his sensibilities, and he soon learned how not to be offended by her comments. Their common exile, their yet unaccomplished dreams, and their shared passion for France drew them closer together. They fell in love, to the great joy of Mary Haskell who, strangely enough, had encouraged this relationship. 'All well for K and M,' she noted with satisfaction in her diary, for this love was far from platonic. It inspired Gibran to write a text entitled, 'From the First Kiss,' in which he wrote,

> It is the first sip from the cup filled by the goddesses with the nectar of Life ... It is the bond that unites the strangeness of the past with the brightness of the future; the link between the silence of the feelings and their song ... It is a word uttered by four lips proclaiming the heart a throne, Love a king, and fidelity a crown ... As the first glance is like a seed sown by the goddess in the field of the human heart, so the first kiss is the first flower at the tip of the branch of the Tree of Life ...

But an unexpected event threw everything out of kilter. According to certain sources,[1] Micheline became pregnant. Her pregnancy was ectopic so she had to have an abortion while keeping this painful event a secret, an event which left its mark on Gibran and affected his future relationships.

In June 1908, Gibran made haste; he packed his bags, and bid his friends goodbye. He wrote to Fred Holland Day to inform him that he was leaving and to express his regret that their relationship had become strained. 'You, dear brother, the first to open the eyes of my childhood to light, will give wings to my manhood,' he wrote with gratitude. On 9 June a farewell dinner was organised in Gibran's honour. Micheline decided to return to France, where she was

---

1. Cf. Robin Waterfield, *Prophet: The Life and Times of Kahlil Gibran*, 1998, p. 108, based on information that appeared in the first Arabic edition of Mikhail Naimy's biography of Gibran.

supposed 'to visit her family'. As for Mary, she promised to go to Paris at the first possible occasion. In New York on 1 July 1908 Gibran boarded *The Rotterdam*. His face held no sadness as he looked at the port he was leaving behind; he knew he would be back.

ﷺ

Paris, at the beginning of the twentieth century, was the city of dreams for artists all over the world. The 'City of Light' was an endless source of creative exuberance. It evoked and awakened the senses, refined aesthetic perception, educated, and nurtured culture. Gibran arrived in Paris on 13 July 1908 and marvelled at the festivities that took place in commemoration of the Fall of the Bastille, which he wrote about enthusiastically to Jamil Malouf. Micheline followed him there and helped him find temporary lodgings in a room on the fifth floor of a building on Avenue Carnot. Shortly afterwards, he moved into a studio at 14 Avenue du Maine[1] in Montparnasse.

Without further ado, the young artist enrolled at l'Académie Julian, the best-known private academy in Paris. Established by Rodolphe Julian, this institution boasted among its alumni Matisse, Bonnard and Léger. It provided students with a 'useful method to start out an artistic career. For a modest amount, it provided them with a model, an education, experience, and contacts without requiring particular skills upon registration.'[2] He also enrolled as an auditor at l'Ecole des Beaux-Arts on Rue Bonaparte, and yielded willingly to the ritual of ragging. 'At the ceremony students had prepared to receive new recruits. I had to drink like everyone else. Some people fell asleep,

1. A commemorative plaque has been placed on the façade of the building to remind people that Gibran, 'Lebanese-American painter and poet', once lived there.
2. John Milner, *Ateliers d'artistes: Paris, capitale des arts à la fin du XIXe siècle*, éd. du May, 1990, p. 18.

others got sick, but I felt nothing. I was rather cheerful and had a good time.'

A few days later, Mary Haskell and her father arrived in Paris. Gibran was very happy to see his protectress again and eager to ask news about Mariana, who did not know how to write. But he could not really benefit from her presence; her father followed her everywhere, and her old Parisian friends monopolised her.

Forlorn after Mary's departure for Boston and Micheline's for Nevers, where her parents lived, Gibran fell sick. But once he was cured, thanks to the care of Lebanese friends, the Rohayems, he went back to the Academy. 'I am painting or I am learning how to paint,' he wrote to Mary. 'It will take me a long time to paint as I want to, but it is beautiful to feel the growth of one's own vision of things ... Now I am beginning to understand things and people through my eyes. My memory seems to keep the shapes and colors of personalities and of objects.'

Micheline went back to the United States and, hoping to make her dream come true by finding her niche on the stage, she settled in New York.[1] 'She should not stay, and I should not ask her to stay,' declared Gibran, who did not want to become an obstacle to his friend's career. The young man took refuge in the memory of Mary, his confidante. The separation made her more charming and made his heart grow fonder of her. He wrote to her nostalgically, with an affection bordering on love, 'When I am unhappy, dear Mary, I read your letters. When the mist overwhelms the "I" in me, I take two or three letters out of the little box and reread them. They remind me of my true self. They make me overlook all that is not high and beautiful in life. Each and every one of us, dear Mary, must have a resting place

---

1. Emilie Michel played a small role in *Little Town of Bethlehem*, performed in the Garden Theater, 17 January to 16 April 1910.

somewhere. The resting place of my soul is a beautiful grove where my knowledge of you lives.'

The tone became more intimate, and their feelings seemed to grow warmer. At a distance, Gibran allowed his feelings to flow easily. As with Posy and May, his future correspondent in Cairo, it was his pen that guided his heart. This gave rise to passionate letters whose lyricism sometimes overrode his sincerity.

Luckily, the absence of Mary and Micheline was compensated for by the company of his old school friend, Yusuf Huwayyik. Yusuf, born the same year as Gibran, had first gone to Rome and then come to Paris to learn the art of painting and sculpture. He was unpretentious and liked socialising and having fun. He was not a dreamer and did not have a tormented soul like Gibran. Yusuf was a regular customer at cafés and considered 'sitting in Dôme an art in itself'. On the other hand, Gibran shied away from noisy places, did not like dancing, and preferred, like Balzac, his role-model, walking along the banks of the River Seine and wandering through the night in the streets of old Paris. But the two companions got along well and spent two unforgettable years in France, which Huwayyik wrote about in a journal. Much later, recollecting this period, Gibran told Yusuf, 'Every night, my spirit travels to Paris and wanders through its streets. And every morning, I wake up thinking about the days we spent amidst the temples of art and the world of dreams.'

In a letter to Mary he wrote, 'There are times when I leave work with the feelings of a child who is sent to bed early.' He was impatient; after only a few months at the Académie Julian, he decided to drop out. Yusuf recalled, 'He was bothered by the mess. He found the advice of his teacher, Jean-Paul Laurens, totally useless.' Should one be surprised? Jean-Paul Laurens (1838–1921), who decorated the Panthéon, the Capitole de Toulouse and the Hôtel de Ville of Paris, was considered one of the last historical painters. Obviously, his style could not win over the romantic spirit of Gibran. Where was he to go?

At the beginning of February 1909, the young artist found a new teacher, Pierre Marcel-Béronneau, a mystic painter, a disciple of Gustave Moreau, who taught a class of twelve students whom he had working on nudes and draped models. 'He is a great artist and a wonderful painter as well as a mystic,' said Gibran. 'The Minister of Culture bought a number of his paintings, and he is known in the art world as "the painter of Salomé". The other day, I took two or three little items to show him. He looked at them for a long time and then, after a few encouraging words, we had a lengthy private conversation. "Let time do its job; don't try to give expression to your thoughts and ideas just yet. Try to go through the entire repertoire of painting."' As might be expected, these words fell on deaf ears; the impetuous Gibran was keen on knowledge and creation. Wanting to go too far too fast, he did not know how to wait. Judging that he had already learned everything his teacher had to offer, he ended up dropping his classes.

He and Yusuf then started going to the Académie Colarossi, run by an Italian named Caterina. This art school, at 10 Rue de la Grande-Chaumière, hosted Camille Claudel and a number of other foreign artists, like the Canadian Jean-Paul Lemieux, Suzor-Côté, Francesco Iacurto and the German Herbert Fiedler, who had come to Paris to develop their art. The Académie specialised in drawings of nude models, but Gibran preferred working alone and freely in his own studio, visiting exhibitions and museums 'to keep up with the artistic scene'. He gave drawing lessons to five students twice a week to earn a little money and then threw himself into a rather demanding project. He planned a series of portraits of famous contemporary people. He started with 'The Temple of Art', the portrait of Paul Bartlett, the American sculptor who had made the statue of La Fayette displayed at the entrance of the Louvre. He followed that with portraits of Edmond Rostand, Claude Debussy, Auguste Rodin and Henri Rochefort, the famous pamphleteer. Gibran's list of portraits is quite impressive. Did he really meet these people 'for only thirty minutes', as he claimed to Mary, or was he able to draw them from memory or based on their photographs? Difficult to tell.

To quench their thirst for knowledge, Gibran and Yusuf went to the Louvre as if on a pilgrimage. They spent hours going all over the vast rooms of the museum. Then they went to enjoy the lawn, trees, flowers and bustling of the Luxemburg Gardens. There, they exchanged opinions about the great artists: Dante, Balzac, Voltaire and Rousseau. At the Panthéon, a short distance from the Luxembourg Gardens, Gibran stood in awe of the fresco of Saint Geneviève, a work by Puvis de Chavannes, who ended up influencing Gibran's painting to some extent.[1] 'Is there deeper serenity than the one you read in his face?' he asked his friend. Sometimes, they went for coffee at La Closerie des Lilas, had lunch at Madame Baudet's restaurant on the corner of Rue Léopold-Robert and Boulevard Raspail, or admired the dancer Isadora Duncan at the Châtelet Theatre. One day, a friend, Dr Gaspard, invited them to the Institut Pasteur. Gibran was impressed. 'Don't you realise that scientists have made more progress than the artists and men of letters?' he asked Yusuf.

Several young ladies, especially foreigners, flitted around the two young 'Parisians'. There was Olga, a Russian student taking French literature courses at the Sorbonne who, as a child, had sat on Tolstoy's knees and played with his beard. Then there were Suzanne and Lia, two Romanian Jews, Rosina the Italian with the golden hair, who considered Botticelli her soul mate, the French Martine, who

---

1. An exhibition at the Plazzo Grassi in Venice (February–June 2002) presented Puvis de Chavannes (1824–98) as one of the giants of modern art and as an artist who inspired Picasso, Gauguin and Matisse.

was fascinated by the question of God's existence, and Marguerite, the dancer at the Moulin Rouge. Yusuf allowed himself to become engulfed by these 'muses' and tried to seduce them, whereas Gibran, no doubt thinking about Mary, kept a certain distance from these women who called him the 'prince' but who could never understand his prophetic comments. Taking advantage of Charlotte Teller's visit to Paris, he showed her his new work and spent a week's holiday with her in Versailles. She inspired him to do a new portrait, but he did not finish it as she would not hold still long enough because 'she had too many dreams and was always running after her own shadow'.

All these activities, these distractions and these acquainttances did not fulfil Gibran. The death of his father, which he learned about in a letter from Bsharri, drove him into deep grief. On 23 June 1909, he wrote to Mary, 'My dear Mary, I have lost my father ... He died in the old house where he was born sixty five years ago ... His friends wrote saying that he blessed me before the end came ... I cannot help but see the dim, sad shadows of the bygone days when he and my mother and my brother and my young sister lived and smiled before the face of the sun. Where are they now? ... Are they together? Do they remember the past as we do? Are they near this world of ours or are they far far away? I know, dear Mary, that they live. They live a life more real, more beautiful than ours. They are nearer to God than we are.'

Gibran, constantly in doubt, asked Yusuf, 'What have we accomplished so far?' or 'When will the East be forced to start thinking? Who will force it to think?' Once, when he did not have enough money to travel and discover the artistic marvels of Italy, he declared fatalistically, 'Damn money! It is an obstacle between man and his faith.' The young man was ambitious and idealistic; he imagined he could change the world and tried to convert other people to his ideas and theories on art, God and nature. Yusuf once said, 'I remember Gibran's state of mind. He dragged his feet on the cold ground while his soul soared in the infinite.' Tormented, Gibran, bogged down with life, smoked a lot, drank many cups of coffee a day, read and reread Gide, Rilke, Tolstoy and Nietzsche, who according to Yusuf, was a 'grumpy philosopher'. Gibran wrote Arabic texts that his entourage deemed 'sad and didactic'. He discovered Ernest Renan, whose bold thoughts intrigued Gibran. Renan dedicated his book, *The Life of Jesus*, to his sister Henriette, who was buried in Lebanon, a country which he himself had visited.

> At the moment I am reading Renan. I like him because he loved and understood Jesus. He saw him in the light of day, not at dusk ... My ultimate hope is to be able to paint the life of Jesus like no one has ever before been able to paint it. My life would find no better peace than in the personality of Jesus.

On 13 February 1909, he published 'The Day I Was Born', a long prose poem dedicated to 'MEH', on the first page of the newspaper *al-Mohajer*. In it he is melancholic and talks about death and his love for life, freedom and the happiness of mankind. He started the draft of a novel which aimed at showing that man, wherever he is, can be in touch with God without having recourse to temples and priests, and that all religions emanate from one single source. His main character, Khalil Ibn Salem, sees the face of God in nature and listens to the birds and waterfalls singing His glory. He believes in Jesus, Buddha and Moses, and affirms that all those who show man the road leading to perfection are emanated from the Grand Spirit of God.[1] But he gave up that novel to work on his manuscript *So That The Universe Might Be Good*, the embryo of *The Prophet*, and to continue working on a novel called *Broken Wings*, the story of a love imprisoned by the traditions of the ecclesiastic power. In addition, one of his stories,

---

1.   Jean-Pierre Dahdah, *Gibran, une biographie*, Albin Michel, 1994, p. 208.

'Martha the Banaise', from the anthology entitled *Nymphs of the Valley*, was translated into French by Michel Bitar (professor of Arabic at the Sorbonne) and appeared in a collection included in Issue 10 of the magazine *Les Mille Nouvelles Nouvelles,* where he is introduced as 'a young Arab writer who writes stories to plead causes such as the Eastern woman's plight and break the religious yoke in Lebanon.' Being included in the same anthology as Chekhov made Gibran very proud.

At the time, following the revolution of the Young Turks against the Ottoman rule of Sultan Abdul-Hamid II, a number of Syrio-Lebanese dissidents took refuge in Paris. Secret societies came into existence and defended the cause of Arab nationalism calling for self-rule in the Ottoman-occupied countries. Among the better-known militants was Chukri Ghanem, poet and playwright, author of a play entitled *Antar*, which was a success at the Odéon theatre. Gibran moved in these circles who demanded political rights for the Arabs living under the Ottoman yoke, the recognition of Arabic as the official language, the effective participation of the Arabs in the central administration of the Ottoman Empire, and the introduction of radical reforms at the heart of that administration. Three years later, Gibran refused to attend an Arab congress designed to study a plan of autonomy for the countries occupied by the Ottomans, under the pretext that the Arabs should revolt for their own freedom, and that it was unwise to use diplomatic means to appeal to European powers. This vision was not shared by his fellow countrymen. It is interesting to note that Amin Rihani took the trip from New York to Paris to represent the Syrio-Lebanese emigrants at that congress.

Eager to expose his painting, Gibran got himself invited to the Salon de Printemps, one of the most prestigious annual exhibitions in Paris. The young painter knew that the time to return to Boston was imminent, and he was bent on participating in the Salon before leaving the City of Light. Of the three works he submitted, the one that was accepted by the jury of the Société Nationale des Beaux-Arts was *Autumn*, which depicted Rosina half naked, holding her golden hair in her right hand. 'Through her stature, the colors and the background, she spoke of the melancholy that interposed itself between the joys and sadness of winter,' explained Gibran. Unluckily, on the day of the hanging, it was not placed in the big exhibition room, but in a narrow hallway at the Grand Palais. Gibran was fuming; he knew that Rodin, the great Rodin, was going to visit the exhibition. If his painting was in a corner, Rodin might not notice it or be able to admire it and ask about the artist. Yusuf came to the rescue of his friend and bribed the curator, who agreed to move the painting to a more prominent place in the bigger exhibition hall.

The following day, Auguste Rodin, surrounded by a flock of perfumed women wearing long dresses and big, flowery hats, came to the exhibition. Gibran saw the septuagenarian with the white beard as he was approaching. Quivering with emotion but taking his courage in both hands, he approached Rodin, greeted him, and with a tremulous voice, said a few words to him. According to Gibran himself, he told Rodin he wanted to show him his painting in the hope that acknowledgment from him would have an impact in the United States, but that Rodin was in a hurry. He stopped for a moment in front of the painting of our young artist, nodded his head, and continued his tour.

In June 1910, Amin Rihani was passing through Paris. Amin Rihani was born in 1876 in Freikeh, a little village in Mount Lebanon whose residents lambasted the activities of the Ottoman occupiers and the behaviour of the clergy. Gibran appreciated the boldness of his ideas. Amin, Yusuf and Gibran rented a carriage and went for long rides in Paris. 'The Father, the Son, and the Holy Ghost,' laughed Rihani, smiling. In the evening Amin and Yusuf, leaving Gibran in his new studio, on Rue du Chereche Midi, went to the Moulin Rouge to admire 'the swirling, scantily dressed women'. The next day, opting for a more serious programme of activity, they spent three hours at the Louvre.

A few days later, Rihani and Gibran went to London. Gibran made a point of seeing the Turner paintings at the Tate Gallery as well as those of Watts and Rossetti. He went with his friend to the home of Thomas Power O'Conner, the Irish nationalist, who showed them around the British parliament. They sent Yusuf a strange letter. It was written jointly by them, and they had alternated writing the lines of the letter. 'We are in a city draped with dark, black clouds, and we look like the birds from the south lost in a northern storm.'

At the end of this trip, Rihani left for New York. Emilie Michel, for her part, made the journey in the opposite direction; she returned to Paris. As Broadway luck had not shone down on her, she needed consolation, which Gibran was more than ready to give her. 'In fact, she suffered a lot, but she was so brave that she kept her nerve. She is still considering going back to the stage and its glory, but right now she knows the darker side of theater life. I hope she will overcome all of this.' Gradually, though, the strength of their relationship subsided. Their passion had only lasted a few months, enough to fuel his inspiration and spur him into doing several paintings of her and saying about her, 'She will always be unique; she will always remain beautiful.' On 1 October 1914, the Frenchwoman ended up marrying a lawyer, Lamar Hardy, advisor to the mayor of New York, John Mitchell.[1] In September 1931, only five months after Gibran's death, she developed a long, debilitating sickness, taking with her her lost

---

1. Laram Hardy was born on 29 May 1879 and died in 1950. He was the son of William Harris Hardy, juror and founder of the cities of Gulfport, Laurel and Hattiesburg in Mississippi. From 1935 to 1939 he was District Attorney of southern New York City..

illusions and broken dreams. She had one child, a daughter born 16 August 1915, whom she named Micheline.[1]

Yusuf Huwayyik went on a trip that took him to Germany, Austria, Turkey, Greece and Italy. Along the way, he wrote to Gibran regularly. Gibran, for his part, was preparing six paintings that he was planning to exhibit in October in the Salon of the Union Internationale des Beaux-Arts, to which he had been officially invited. But weary of his precarious situation, Gibran ended up abandoning the project, and on 22 October 1910 he returned to the United States. According to his friend Yusuf, 'his stay in Paris did not hold any significance in the artistic dimension.' This opinion, however, is debatable. When Charlotte Teller was in Paris, she wrote to Mary, 'His work shows an immense improvement. He has touched reality and he has learned how to draw. His color sense is his own and I feel that his whole nature has matured and strengthened in this year.' His intellectual enrichment and the humanistic breath now a part of his work, his mastering of the pictorial technique and especially oil painting, from wash to aquarelles, his perfection of portrait art, and his political involvement are enough to declare his stay in Paris decisive. Whatever the future held, Gibran would retain an emotional memory of this period, as evidenced by the letter he sent to Yusuf from Boston, dated 19 December 1911.

> Yusuf, my brother,
> Happy is he who can own a spot in Paris. Happy is he who can walk along the banks of the Seine and rummage through the shelves of second-hand booksellers to look for old books and drawings. Here, in this city [Boston], I have many friends and family... Yet I am not happy ... Remember me when you go to

---

1. Micheline Hardy, the daughter of Emilie Michel, was married on 7 September 1945 to William Brauson Claggett and had two daughters, Susan Sommer Claggeth, born in 1947, and Barbara Hardy Claggett, born in 1950.

the Louvre and stand in front of the Goddess of Victory. My homage to the Mona Lisa.

A few months later, on 23 April 1912, he wrote to his friend Jamil Malouf, who was in France at the time:

Paris! Paris, theater of arts and thought, source of imagination and dreams! In Paris I was reborn, and it is there that I would like to spend the rest of my life ... I will return to Paris to nourish my starving heart and quench my thirsting soul. I will return to eat of its divine bread and drink its magical wine.

Gibran never made it back to Paris and never saw his native homeland, Lebanon, again. Deprived of the places he loves, can an artist be happy?

SEVEN

'Beloved Mary'

*U*pon his arrival in Boston on 1 November, 1910 Gibran hurried over to his sister Mariana's house. He had not seen her for two years, so it was a moving reunion of the only survivors in the family that had suffered so much loss. He then went to see Mary, who received him with open arms and told him she had just lost her father. Worried about keeping him under her control, she told him that she had decided to continue giving him the seventy-five dollars she was sending him monthly throughout his stay in Paris. She also advised him to rent larger accommodation so that he would have no constraints working on his art. Gibran jumped at the opportunity and rented a house on 18 West Cedar Street on Beacon Hill. The bond between Mary and her protégé inevitably became stronger. He showed her the drawings he had made in Paris; she corrected his English diction. They went out together frequently, visiting the Museum of Fine Arts and going to concerts or the theatre. Gibran shared with her his fascination with Jesus, 'the most sublime of all human creatures'. Obviously influenced by the ideas of Renan, he told her that he had read everything he could find on Jesus and that all his life, his admiration for him had not stopped growing. He considered him to be the greatest of all artists and poets, and that calling him God would actually diminish him, as in being God, his marvellous words would seem small, but as a man, it was poetry of the purest kind.

The tenth of December that year introduced a new element into the Mary–Gibran relationship. It was the evening of Mary's thirty-seventh birthday, and Gibran was having dinner at her house. All of a sudden, at midnight, he took her hand, held it to his lips, and declared in a very solemn voice that he loved her and wanted to marry her. She was startled but remained calm, explaining that the difference in their ages would make marriage impossible for them. In her journal, she wrote that although she knew their love was mutual, she was afraid that the age difference would eventually pose an insurmountable obstacle and for now, at least, would spoil their friendship.[1]

Gibran was just as wounded by the unexpected rejection as he was by the unconvincing pretext Mary gave him for that rejection. Later, he wrote to her, 'I came back from Paris full of this. I went and gave you my heart so simply, so frankly, so sincerely, so wholly. I was just a boy putting all I was and all I had into your hands. And you met me so coldly, so quizzically.' And in another letter, he wrote, 'Then the very day after I spoke to you of marriage you began to hurt me.'

Overrun with guilt or regret, Mary soon changed her mind. She decided to say 'yes' to Gibran, who became hopeful again. A few days later, she changed her mind yet again. This vacillation was difficult to explain. Should one believe her when she said she felt she would never be able to live up to the love he deserved? Her ambivalent relationship with Charlotte and liaisons with other women, to which she confessed in a letter dated 19 December 1914, might serve to explain her behaviour. Or was it the notion of marrying a foreigner that dissuaded her? Was she afraid that when her brother came for an impromptu visit she would not be able to hide her embarrassment? Whatever the reasons, Mary knew she was guilty. In a letter dated July

---

1. According to Naimy, Mary asked Gibran, 'Is your body free from all illnesses?' which hurt his feelings (Mikhaïl Naimy, *Gibran Khalil Gibran*, 1934, p. 123).

1915, she confessed, 'Kahlil, I have done you all the wrong I could do. You took me to the very tenderest center of your heart and it was from there that I gave you every blow and every wound ... My soul treated you like an inferior ... I have been in one long, continued sin against you ... through all these nearly five years.' But what use was the belated confession? He was weary of her equivocation. ('Something in me was dying day by day,' he told Mary. 'I was constantly being tortured. If you had continued like that, I would have ended up hating you.') In an attempt to sublimate his disappointment, Gibran buried himself in his work. He took Mariana and two of his cousins as models and did portraits of several Bostonian personalities. He sketched a new self-portrait in oils: in it his face is turned three-quarters to the right with a woman (Mary?) in the background holding a crystal ball. He did not stop writing and sent to Nageeb Diab, the director of the New York newspaper *Mir'at al-Gharb* ('The Mirror of the West') a virulent article entitled, 'We and You', dedicated as usual to 'M.E.H.':

> You have built the Pyramids upon the hearts of slaves, but the Pyramids stand now upon the sand, commemorating to the Ages our immortality and your evanescence ... You have built Babylon upon the bones of the weak, and erected the palaces of Nineveh upon the graves of the miserable. Babylon is now but the footprint of the camel upon the moving sand of the desert, and its history is repeated to the nations who bless us and curse you ... You crucified Jesus and stood below Him, blaspheming and mocking at Him; but at last He came down and overcame the generations, and walked among you as a hero, filling the universe with His glory and His beauty. You poisoned Socrates and stoned Paul and destroyed Ali Talib and assassinated Madhat Pasha, and yet those immortals are with us forever before the face of Eternity.

On Good Friday, he published an article entitled 'The Crucified' which appeared later in *The Tempests*. In it one can see Gibran's attachment to the figure of Jesus and his determination to raise his spirit by meditating on the Nazarene.

> Today, and on the same day of each year, man is startled from his deep slumber and stands before the phantoms of the Ages, looking with tearful eyes toward Mount Calvary to witness Jesus the Nazarene nailed on the Cross ... For centuries Humanity has been worshipping weakness in the person of the Savior. The Nazarene was not weak! He was strong and is strong! But the people refuse to heed the true meaning of his strength. Jesus never lived a life of fear, nor did He die suffering or complaining ... He lived as a leader; He was crucified as a crusader; He died with a heroism that frightened His killers and tormenters ... Jesus came not from the heart of the circle of Light to destroy the homes and build upon their ruins the convents and monasteries. He did not persuade the strong man to become a monk or a priest, but He came to send forth upon this earth a new spirit, with power to crumble the foundations of any monarchy built upon human bones and skulls ... He came to demolish the majestic palaces, constructed upon the graves of the weak, and crush the idols, erected upon the bodies of the poor. Jesus was not sent here to teach people to build magnificent churches and temples amidst the cold wretched huts and dismal hovels ... He came to make the human heart a temple, and the soul an altar,and the mind a priest. Forgive the weak who lament Thee today, for they do not know how to lament themselves ... Forgive them, for they do not know that Thou hast conquered death with death and bestowed life upon the dead ...

Still under the influence of the political ideas of the freedom fighters taking refuge in France, Gibran hastened to convince the Lebanese and Syrian communities in Boston to start an organisation to defend the cause of the Arab countries under Ottoman control. The association was created in 1911 and was called 'al-Halaqa al Dahabyia'

(The Golden Circle). The founders decided to keep their activities clandestine and to call the members of this brotherhood 'al-Hurras' (The Guardians), a name inspired by the Masonic lodges. On 25 February 1911, at a large meeting organised by the association, Gibran took the floor and delivered an impassioned speech to the Syrians to beware of the promises of the sultan and to rely on themselves from then on to throw off the Turkish yoke. 'Whoever does not walk with his head held high will remain his own slave, and he who is his own slave cannot walk freely. Freedom is a ray that emanates from the inside and not one that shines from without,' he declared. This speech, published in the newspaper *Mir'at al-Gharb* that March, turned loyalist newspapers in Syria and Egypt against him. Two years later *al-Sa'ih* ('The Tourist') published an article of his under the title 'Open Letter from a Christian Poet to Muslims'. In it, he called for all Muslims to rise against the occupation, as the Ottoman state was responsible for the decadence of Islamic civilisation. That, too, elicited the wrath of the Ottomans and their allies, 'I am Lebanese and proud of that. I am not an Ottoman and I'm also proud of that. I am Christian and proud of that. But I love the Arab Prophet and I honor his name; I cherish the glory of Islam and worry that it will fade ... Some people call me a renegade, as I hate the Ottoman state and wish for its eclipse. I answer them that I hate the Ottoman state because I love Islam and wish it would regain its glory.' Driven by prophetic intuition, Gibran thought that if the Syrians did not revolt, they would be driven back onto the mercy of the imperialist forces that coveted the region. 'The Christian that I am, who placed Jesus in one half of his heart and Mohammed in the other half, assures you that if Islam does not conquer the Ottoman Empire, the European nations will dominate Islam. If none of you will rise against the internal enemy within this generation, the Levant will fall into the hands of those with fair skin and blue eyes ...'

Artistically speaking, the child of Bsharri was somewhat disgruntled. Boston was too small, too stifling for someone who had lived in Paris and was used to going to grand museums. 'This is a city of mortal silence where nothing is happening ...' Oddly, this attitude is similar to that of Louis Leverett, Henry James's hero in *The Point of View*, who having left the City of Light for Boston wrote to Harvard Tremont, 'I am a stranger here ... This country is very cold, very harsh, and very empty. I think of Paris, so rich and warm.'[1] He who thought of the French experience as 'the first step on the ladder that links earth to the sky' felt the need to change locale to continue to grow. He wrote to Amin Rihani, 'I am like a ship, whose sail is torn by the winds and whose prow is shattered by the breaker waves, coming and going in the midst of the furious tides in the storm.'

Anxious to find a better environment for his artistic output and wanting to take a step back from his indecisive protectress, Gibran chose to go to New York. His sister Mariana pleaded with him to change his mind, but her efforts were in vain. Mary was sad to see him moving away from her. Deep down, her feelings were in disarray. She had decided not to marry him, but at the same time, convinced that his success was now imminent and that he was the 'ultimate finger of God', she was determined to support him through thick and thin in his artistic career. Without further delay, she asked Charlotte Teller, who was passing through Boston and had seen Gibran again, to help him find an apartment near her in Manhattan and urged her to continue posing for the artist.

Gibran, who naively hoped that Mary would leave her school to follow him, endured another rejection. His pride hurt a second time, he packed up and left with no regrets, taking the manuscript of *Broken Wings* and a copy of Nietzsche's *Thus Spake Zarathustra* with him.

---

1.   Quoted by Jean Meral, *Paris dans la littérature américaine*, ed. CNRS, 1983, p. 91.

EIGHT

New York

*A*ccording to Paul Claudel, who arrived in New York in 1893, 'the lower part of the city that you first see upon arrival looks like an extravagant cramming together of towers, domes, enormous buildings of ten, fifteen, and twenty-five stories, banks, newspapers, and office buildings. For the stranger who lands there, unaware of what is going on or why, the first days are staggering.'[1] From the outset, Gibran understood that New York was not a place for resting. He started by visiting the Metropolitan Museum of Art, which left him marvelling. He met the Lebanese community of the city and, thanks to Mary's letters of introduction, several eminent New Yorkers. He found his old friend, Amin Rihani. 'How happy I will be when fate throws us together in the same city again!' he had written to him before his trip. He painted his portrait and moved into his apartment building for a little while.

On 1 June, Mary arrived in New York. When she met up with Gibran, she found him working on a new painting entitled *Isis*, for which he had used Charlotte Teller as a model. Mary wondered

---

1.   François Angelier, *Paul Claudel*, Pygmalion/Gérard Watelet, 2000, p. 79.

what role this woman was playing in the life of her artist. It is true that she had done everything to throw Charlotte, whom she looked after and loved, into his arms, but the real nature of their relationship eluded her. She convinced herself that she would have to accept that Charlotte was giving him carnal love, something she herself could not do at that point. The truth of the matter was that Gibran was fascinated by Charlotte as he was painting her, but that there was no real chemistry there. She gave herself to Amin Rihani, who had fallen under the charm of this mysterious woman, but she ended up marrying Gilbert Hirsch[1] a few months later.

During Mary's brief stay, she and Gibran visited the city museums, the Cathedral of St John the Divine, and Columbia University. In the evening, when they were not reading *Thus Spake Zarathustra* together, Gibran enjoyed drawing sketches of Keats, Shelley, Rodin and Dante, among others.

When Mary went back to Boston, Gibran went along too. He wanted to see his sister again, and Mary wanted to get ready for her vacation out West, where she enjoyed her favorite sport, hiking. That is when Mary suggested giving him a lump sum of 5,000 dollars, rather than sending him monthly instalments, with the view of giving him more breathing room. He accepted but insisted on leaving her everything he owned in his will as a sign of appreciation. And, putting his words into action, he took a blank piece of paper and drew up his will – even though he was only twenty-eight years old. It was an astonishing will which included all, or almost all, his friends. He left his paintings and drawings to Mary, or in the event of her death before his, to Fred Holland Day. His literary manuscripts were to go to his sister with advice to consult Amin Rihani and the journalists Nageeb

---

1. Charlotte Teller Hirsch went to Europe in 1922 and settled in France. She continued to write using the pseudonym 'John Brangwyn' and published *Everybody's Paris* (1935) and *Reasons for France* (1939). She died in Paris in 1954.

Diab and Amin Gorayeb before publication of any kind. The letters in Arabic and French he had received were for Yusuf Huwayyik; to the library in Bsharri he donated the books he owned in Lebanon, and those found in Boston to the Golden Circle. Could anyone have been fairer?

A real workaholic ('I wish I could be several Kahlils,' he would sigh), Gibran took advantage of the summer to carry out several projects. He finished *Broken Wings*, put the finishing touches to *Isis*, started four new paintings, illustrated the autobiography of Amin Rihani, *The Book of Khalid*, and sent two articles, 'Slavery' and 'Son of My Mother', to *Mir'at al-Gharb*. 'Slavery' is a condemnation of the various forms of subjugation of people's will, among which is included the twisted regime that forces a people to abide by laws of a nation other than their own and where the sons of monarchs are crowned even if they are unfit to rule. In 'Son of My Mother' he protests against the passiveness of his fellow countrymen towards the occupier. Gibran's impetuous, virulent tirades are reminiscent of St John the Baptist's and the prophets of the Old Testament. They are commensurate with the political, social and cultural lethargy of the Arab world, dominated by the Ottoman Empire and then by the superpowers.

Gibran went to Boston for short visits. When he was there, he attended a conference given by the Irish poet and playwright, William Butler Yeats, future Nobel Prize winner. At the end of the conference, Yeats agreed to see Gibran. They met on 1 October. Gibran was fascinated by the poet whom he considered 'corrupted by patriotism' and did his portrait. They saw each other again in 1914 at Mrs Ford's dinner and then again in 1920 at the main centre of the Society of Arts and Sciences.

Back in New York, in October 1911 he moved into the Tenth Street

Studio, a red brick building reserved exclusively for artists, on 51 West 10th Street – smack in the middle of Greenwich Village. In that same year, *Broken Wings* was published in Arabic as *Mir'at al-Gharb*. This book, unquestionably the most romantic book Gibran ever wrote, tells the story of a hopeless love. The narrator, an idealist, loves Salma, one of his countrywomen, who is married off against her will to the archbishop's nephew, a dishonest character who wants her only for her money. After the wedding, the narrator and Salma continue to see each other in secret. She falls pregnant and dies just after delivering a stillborn child. The book, one of the first novels in Arabic literature, which had been previously dominated by poetry, contained the germinating seed of Gibran's future style and thought. From a literary point of view, the reader quickly realises that the fictional framework is interrupted by reflective digressions and that the story is merely a pretext for the author to express ideas about which he felt strongly. Among these are the rejection of archaic traditions that bind eastern women, the condemnation of clerical feudalism, death, beauty, revolution, love, motherliness and nature. Broaching the uniqueness of human existence, a recurring theme in his works, he writes, 'Man's life does not commence in the womb and never ends in the grave; and this firmament, full of moonlight and stars, is not deserted by loving souls and intuitive spirits.' He was inspired by Rousseau, whom he admired, to believe that 'man, although born free, remains a slave of the cruelty of laws that his fathers and ancestors laid down.' He also celebrates euphonic beauty and the purity of nature in contrast with the corruption of men. With Mary in mind, he wrote about love, 'It is wrong to think that love comes from long companionship and persevering courtship. Love is the offspring of spiritual affinity and unless that affinity is created in a moment, it will not be created in years or even generations.' On death, he has a dying man say, 'The days of slavery are gone, and my soul seeks the freedom of the skies.' But the novelist does not always manage to hide behind his characters, and when Salma declares that a 'thirsty spirit is grander than the substance quenched by it; a frightened soul is preferable to a pacified body', it is the voice of Gibran that one hears. The literary saving grace of *Broken Wings* is its poetic breath animating the ensemble: metaphors, symbols, present even in the title chapters, spark the imagination of the reader; the rhythm of the sentences is so well cadenced as is only possible in a prose poem, a genre that Gibran introduced to Arabic literature.

On Mary's birthday, Gibran sent her a copy of the book dedicated to her. She had written to him on his birthday, 'Dear Hand, dear Eye, dear Thought, dear Fire, dear Love – Thanks to the bon Dieu who gave you to your mother twenty-nine years ago – and one year drew you and me nearer together.' Rarely has any relationship between man and woman been more ambivalent, more complicated, built with the ebb and flow of domination and adoration, of distance and consuming passion, at the same time Platonic and sensual, expressed in words and in images. It was as if Mary, in writing to Gibran or hiding secret feelings in her diary, possessed him, or as if Gibran, in painting his protectress or in dedicating his books to her, controlled her. Wasn't it André Breton who claimed that 'love is made of words'? On a trip to New York, Mary said one night that she heard a voice calling to her, telling her that Kahlil was running out of patience, that he had to have all or nothing. She interpreted this dream as a sign that she should have sexual relations with him with a view to establishing some kind of balance between the impossibility of marriage to him and the powerful desire that was pushing them together. She ran to her friend to share her vision with him. Gibran categorically rejected this half-baked idea. Perhaps he was thinking of the risks of such a relationship and the abortion Micheline had had to have, if that information was accurate.

'Now I know that you love me,' he murmured.

Mary protested, 'Didn't you know that already?'

'Yes, but not like that. But I cannot accept your proposition. I love you too much to make you my mistress.'

Mary left, ashamed at having been so daring. In the evening, she went back on her promise to visit him with Micheline, who was about to get married. But the next day, she tried again.

'Before returning to Boston, I would like to be yours,' she said urgently.

'I would have liked to say it first,' he retorted bitterly.

'You have always told me that I hold the key in my hands. Today I am giving you that key.'

'But why now?'

'We would never have wanted to talk about it had I not taken the initiative.'

Gibran was angry, 'But I was the first one to have declared my love, to have asked for your hand, and wished that you would come closer to my heart! Now I weary of holding a strong-willed woman.'

It is all there, in the confession of this offended man. By nature, Gibran was touchy and grudging. He forgot neither the rejection of his protectress nor her embarrassment when her brother saw them together. 'It was the determining blow. The man in me had to retreat into self-protection.' Tired of Mary's indecision, he refused to allow her to continue to play with his feelings. Nothing in his behaviour corroborates some biographers' insinuations that he pretended to love her to continue taking advantage of her or that he proposed marriage only to show his gratitude and that in his heart of hearts was hoping she would refuse. The letters of Gibran cannot possibly be hypocritical; they reflected a genuine love. And all things considered, his attitude seemed more sincere than Mary's, who never revealed the real reasons that prevented her from marrying the man she venerated. 'I can no longer stand the uncertainty. You told me so many contradictory things with equal seriousness, and I don't know which version to believe. For months, I have suffered terribly.' Mary was, in fact, much more complicated than one can imagine. Her diary and her letters reveal a woman torn between a frustrated libido and insurmountable taboos, between her attraction to women and her desire for men, between her will to be emancipated and the respect for decorum imposed by her conservative family.

Certain psychoanalysts have interpreted Gibran's attitude towards his friend as an unresolved Oedipus complex, claiming that he was searching for the face of his mother in every woman, so that every romantic relationship was bound to become a source of conflict. On one hand there was desire; on the other the forbidden violation of the sacred temple of his 'mother'. However, this analysis only partially serves to explain Gibran's behaviour as the deadlock with Mary was basically due to her unstable attitude and since otherwise, his relationships with other women were not in conflict, in the psychoanalytical sense of the word. So, why did he not get married? Wanting to hold on to his freedom, traumatised by the incident with Micheline (in her writings, Mary confirmed that he was upset over the negative aftermath of a sexual relationship), let down by Posy and then by Mary ('May God help me against gentle, spoiled women who complain and are filled with self-doubt,' he wrote to Helena Ghostine), Gibran decided never to commit himself again. To justify his decision, he claims, 'If I had a woman and I was writing poems or painting, I might forget about her for days on end. No woman in love would put up with such a husband for long.' Better yet, conceding that 'the most sexual creatures on earth are the creators', he claims to transform the force of his libido into an artistic power. 'I too have a vivid artistic warmth, but I believe that a large part of my power flows into my work ...'

After several futile attempts, Mary finally gave up. From then on, according to her journal, she no longer looked upon Gibran as a friend with whom she was in love, but as a husband with whom she shared a great friendship. But would her mood swings allow her to accept this condition for long? For the young man, in any case, things were clear. 'On the personal, intimate level, my relationship with this woman is impossible. It has to be limited to the sprit and the soul. She hurt me so much that love had to find another form of expression.' Later, he told Mary, 'If we had had a sexual relationship, in time it would have come between us. Our lives are on the same track, and sex has spared us.' In fact, in spite of the caresses and kisses inviting their bodies to unite, they never took that ultimate step.

On 15 April 1912, terrible news shook the world: the *Titanic* sank, and aboard the ship were hundreds of travellers, a large number of whom were Lebanese, crammed in the ship's hold.[1] Gibran was shocked by the news. He spent an almost sleepless night. 'The air was heavy owing to this terrible tragedy at sea,' he wrote. That same day he met Abdul Baha', the son of Baha'Ullah, founder of the Bahai faith, a spiritual movement begun in Iran. It advocated one universal religion, the unity of God, the acknowledgement of all the prophets, inculcated the principle of the Unity and homogeneity of all humankind, called for equality of the sexes, and glorified work. Gibran did a portrait of Abdul Baha' and invited him to speak at the Golden Circle on the unity of religions.[2] Then, he dove back into *So That the Universe Might Be Good*, whose title he changed to *The God of the Island*. What was Gibran like at this point in his life? His physique was similar to that of the people from his village: a tanned complexion,

---

1. Of the eighty-five Lebanese passengers on board, fifty-two died (M. Karma, *The Lebanese on Board the Titanic*, Beirut 2000, p. 43).

2. Starting in April 1912, Abdul Baha' visited over forty cities in Canada and the US and gave over 100 lectures (Christian Cannier, *The Bahais*, ed. Brepols, 1887, p. 27).

a prominent nose, a thick black moustache, bushy arched eyebrows, slightly curly hair and full lips. He had a wide forehead, as majestic as a cupola, with eyelids drooping over vivacious eyes suggesting intelligence. He was short with a powerful neck and strong hands, and his radiant smile gave him deep dimples, lending him the air of an innocent child. His charisma was unfailing. Claude Bragdon[1] reports, 'No matter who is around him, his charm works and makes him the center of attention.' Mary found him 'electrifying, and as volatile as a flame.' He had a rather sad disposition and liked to isolate himself ('Solitude is a silent storm that breaks down all our dead branches') and become immersed in his work. Proud and overly-sensitive, he could not bear to be criticised. Independent and rebellious by nature, he hated all forms of injustice.

One aspect of his character that not many people knew was the finesse of his humour. His correspondence with May Ziadeh, his friend in Cairo, is sprinkled with witticisms. For example, when she reproaches him for preferring blondes to brunettes, he answers her with a prayer, 'O, God, Send one of Your angels to tell May that this servant of yours sings the praises of dark hair as much as he does of fair hair.' In a letter to Mary Haskell dated 21 January 1918 he wrote, 'I am sending two wash drawings. I am sending them just for the color in them – your walls need a touch of color here and there. They are not nude enough to offend any person in Boston – I mean the two drawings, not your walls!' When he found out that his protectress had postponed a trip to Egypt, he declared, 'I am sorry that your trip was postponed. But Egypt has been there for six thousand years; it will stay another six thousand. You will surely get to see it.' Gibran, who was sorry that Jesus's sense of humour went unrecognised, shows a lot of spunk in his aphorisms. 'Those who give you a serpent when you had asked for a fish, may have nothing but serpents to give. It

---

1.   Architect, writer and theosophist (1866-1946).

is then generosity on their part.' Or, 'The most talkative is the least intelligent, and there is hardly a difference between an orator and an auctioneer.' And this unexpected tirade, 'He who would understand a woman, or dissect genius, or solve the mystery of silence is the very man who would wake from a beautiful dream to sit at a breakfast table!' Mary Haskell appreciated that sense of humour. 'Will you make me laugh when we meet in Heaven?' she asked him. Then she wrote in her diary, 'Every time I meet him, even when he is sad, he makes me laugh and laugh.'

Gibran smoked and drank a lot. 'Today,' he wrote to Mary, 'I smoked more than twenty cigarettes. Smoking, for me, is a pleasure, not a compulsive habit ...' At night, to stay up and be able to focus on his work, he drank strong coffee and took cold baths. This unbalanced lifestyle was taking its toll on his body. 'More than forty years are engraved on his face, although he is only thirty-three,' noted Mary. 'His left shoulder, hurt in a childhood accident, is almost paralyzed.'

Over the course of 1913, Gibran met a number of influential personalities in the artistic world of New York, among whom were the poet Witter Bynner, editor of *McClure's Magazine*, and Arthur Bowen Davies, founder of the Association of American Painters and Sculptors and organiser of the International Exhibition of Modern Art, for whom Mary Haskell agreed to pose nude to make her protégé jealous and in the hope of getting a reaction from him. In February, Gibran gave Mary a collection of ten paintings as reimbursement of his debt to her. He wanted to break free from his dependence on her bit by bit, as it was making him uncomfortable. Gibran did not appreciate it when Mary told him, 'I can only stay in touch with you through money.' He replied bitterly, 'Tell me right now what your real aim was in giving me this money, and I will know what to expect. Tell me simply so that I am not misled. Was it a gift, a loan, or a means of strengthening our relationship?'

Once again, Gibran threw himself into his series of portraits, 'The Temple of Art', and finished those of Thomas Edison and Carl Gustave Jung, who had agreed to pose for him. He also met Henri Bergson, who was exhausted by his long trip to the USA and promised to let Gibran do his portrait in Paris. The following year came the turn of General Garibaldi, son of the famous Italian revolutionary, and the 'divine' Sarah Bernhardt. 'She was most gracious,' Gibran wrote to Mary in a letter. 'She spoke with more than delight of her visits to Syria and Egypt. She also said that her mother spoke Arabic and that the music of that language lived and is still living in her soul.' Sarah Bernhardt was no longer very young at sixty-nine but had not lost any of her coquettishness. She agreed to pose for Gibran on condition that he draw her from afar so that the details of her aging face would not show. When he finished the drawing, at the end of the session, the actress leaned over to look at her portrait; she liked it. Just a few wrinkles to eliminate, the full-lipped mouth to redo ... Gibran knew that 'Sarah Bernhardt was difficult to satisfy and to understand. It was difficult to be around her. She had a temper. One had to treat her like a queen, or else one was finished.' For his patience and docility, he was duly rewarded: on leaving, she stretched out her left hand for him to kiss; a sign of honour she bestowed only upon those of whom she approved.

In April 1913, a new magazine, *al-Founoun* ('The Arts'), owned by Naseeb Arida came out in New York. Gibran eagerly contributed to this publication; he published various articles and prose poems in it. His style is recognisable in all of them: the fluidity of his sentences, his use of parallelism, repetition, antonymy, his profusion of allusions and allegorical images charge his writing with emotion and poetry. In this same magazine, he wrote various literary studies about grand mystics such as al-Ghazali and Ibn al-Farid.

Where did Gibran acquire such a fascination with Sufism?

Introduced at a very young age to the works of the Sufi poets, he was conscious of their impact on him. Likewise, the symbol of the 'winged self' and the image of wings, which recur as much in his writings as in his drawings, seem to jump straight out of the following text by Rumi:

> How could the soul not take flight
> When from the glorious Presence
> A soft call flows as sweet as honey
> Comes right up to her and whispers,
> "Rise up now, come away."
> Fly away, fly away bird to your native home,
> You have leapt free of the cage
> Your wings are flung back in the wind of God.
> Leave behind the stagnant and marshy waters,
> Hurry, hurry, hurry O bird, to the Source of Life! [1]

Similarly, the image of the sun, ever-present in Gibran's work, finds its source in Sufi symbolism, where the daytime star, considered a spirit that illuminates the world, is an incarnation of divine uniqueness. 'The sun,' explains René Guénon, 'is established as the perfect symbol of the Principle One, the necessary Being. He alone is self-sufficient in his total bliss, and the existence and the subsistence of all things depend entirely on him; outside of him there would be mere nothingness.' [2] Other expressions, other images, inspired by Sufism, like spiritual hunger, nostalgia, the veil, the *nay* ... all of them are found in Gibran, proof that 'if his works are not to be considered as essays of faithful representation of the Sufi doctrine, they express nonetheless his interpretation of the Sufi concepts, seen through the prism of his own poetic sensibility.' [3]

---

1.   Eva de Vitray-Meyerovitch, *Anthology of Sufism*, Albin Michel, 1995, p. 52.
2.   Malek Chebel, *Dictionary of Islamic Symbols*, Albin Michel, 1995, p. 394.
3.   Antoine Ghattas Karam, *La vie et l'œuvre littéraire de Gibran Khalil Gibran*, 1981, p. 242.

Under the influence of the Sufi masters, Gibran is obsessed by the notion of internal purification extending to all levels of the human psyche: the purification of the soul (*nafs*) is achieved by penitence and asceticism; the purification of the heart (*qalb*) by solitude, retreat and meditation; and purification of the spirit (*ruh*) by faith and love directed towards union with God.[1] Throughout his existence, Gibran aspired to purity but was ceaselessly thwarted by the hectic lifestyle of New York and Boston and by what he prudishly refers to as 'life's desires'. His spiritual retreats were too short for his liking, and his incessant longing for his homeland was perhaps only a desire to escape towards places more conducive to meditation. He shared with the Sufis, influenced no doubt by Neo-Platonic and Buddhist ideals, the notions of the uniqueness of existence (*ahadiat al woujoud*) and the union with God.[2]

> *Listen, o Beloved!*
> *I am the Reality of the world,*
> *I am the center and the circumference,*
> *I am the parts and the whole*
> *Loved one, let us approach union*
> *Let us go hand in hand,*
> *Let us enter in the presence of Truth,*
> *Let Truth be our judge*
> *And stamp forever*
> *Her seal on Our union.*[3]

Gibran held al-Ghazali in great esteem. 'In al-Ghazali I found what makes him a golden chain that links his predecessors, the mystics of India, to other theologians who came after him. Al-Ghazali's

---

1.   Jean Chevalier, *Le Soufisme*, PUF, p. 97.
2.   Djamchid Mortazavi, *Le Secret de l'Unité dans l'ésotérisme iranien*, Dervy-Livres, 1988, ch. 1.
3.   Ibn Arabi, in *Anthology of Sufism*, p. 46.

inclinations are reminiscent of what Buddhist thinking had accomplished up till then; and in the recent works of Spinoza or William Blake, we find traces of these feelings.' Convinced, like a great Sufi thinker, that the world is the mirror of God, he subscribed to the notion that 'divine mercy conferred upon the visible world a relationship with the world of the celestial kingdom, and for this reason, there is not a single thing in the world of senses that is not a symbol of something in the other world. There is only one Reality, the unique divinity; to become aware of this is to attain that union ...'[1]

According to Gibran, Ibn al-Farid (another Sufi) was 'a poet of divine inspiration. His thirsty soul drank from enough wine of the spirit to become drunk; from then on, it floated, flying over the physical world, where the dreams of poets, the sighs of lovers, and desires of the mystics drifted. Then, surprised to return to its senses, it came back to the visible world to register what it had seen and heard.' Gibran shared with the poet the theme of a mystical desire to melt into the Spirit. ('My soul has never stopped feeding on spiritual desires,' says Ibn al-Farid.) He also shared the idea that all things in the real world are one and are only attributes of the Divine Essence, 'All beings in their own language, if only you listen, bring an eloquent testimony to my unity ... Everything in me looks for my Whole and goes towards it.'[2] Gibran could not help being captivated by the duality of human-divine love, which Ibn al-Farid presents, as do most other Sufi poets, as a God becoming 'She', the divine lover. In Sufism, earthly love appears to be a means of attaining divine love and reaching Union. This is illustrated in the pictorial works of Gibran, where the theme is shown by a proliferation of uniting couples, with

---

1.   Ghazali, in *Anthology of Sufism*, p. 302.

2.   Ibn al-Farid, *La Grande Taiyya*, translated and presented by Claudine Chonez, Différence ed., 1987, pp. 44–45.

their arms crossed or embracing, in the middle of nature or under the approving eye of the crucifix.

Wanting to create a more propitious framework for meditation, on 1 May 1913, Gibran moved to the fourth (top) floor of the building in which he was living. The new apartment, more spacious and better lit than the previous one, could easily accommodate his studio. From then on, the place that Rihani described as 'a salon dedicated to thought, art, and the beautiful' and which encompassed easels, paintings, books, documents, antiques and statues, was nicknamed 'As Saoumaa' ('The Hermitage'). Rarely was a place better named. In this phase of his life, where mysticism started to override his bellicose attitudes, the artist wanted to become more and more entrenched in silence. 'He is free when he is alone,' noted Mary, who knew him better than anyone else. 'I would like to be a hermit,' he wrote to her, thinking undoubtedly about the ones he saw as a child in the monastery of Qoshaya. And he added, in another one of his letters, 'I like being where my books and paintings are.'

On 25 October, Mary secretly underwent treatment in a medical establishment. Some authors claim that she was suffering from painful neuritis; others say she had an abortion, having become pregnant by the painter Davies, who had asked her to pose for him.[1] This would explain Gibran's bitterness and rejection of her. Whatever credit can be accorded to the stories about her pregnancy or her venereal disease (Gibran's letters dated 26 October and 30 October lead one to think something unexpected had taken place), it remains true that the disharmony between Gibran and Mary had started well before that.

On 16 November, Mary wrote Gibran a letter that summarised perfectly the path of the artist. 'And I am very conscious of your suffering, even when you do not speak of it. When I think of the

---

1.   On this opinion: Chikhani, *Religion et société dans l'œuvre de Gibran*, Lebanese University Press, Beirut 1997.

burdens you carry, the work that hurts like childbirth labor and never stops, the two arts, the two tongues, the two worlds (hemispheres), the two eras, of present and future, the loneliness, and of the handicaps under which you must live the life that is enough for two geniuses; lack of means, lack of robust health, lack of the aids of home and background and native surroundings ... and occasional stabs out of trusted darkness ... so that your life moves from one set of pains into another ... when I think of all these things, it hurts beyond hurt. At last I remember God ... Measureless are your pains, and the vast outlines of the work you feel growing in you, the pains are small in proportion to what is being born – and the real work is beyond what in this generation or perhaps for many generations even you can realise. Only the future can show its scope.'

Mary believed in Gibran, and it was her faith in him that gave the artist wings.

NINE

May

'*M*ay' was the nickname of a tormented woman who, like the sea, was by turn calm and transparent, and turbulent. May Ziadeh[1] was born in Nazareth in 1886. Her father was a Lebanese teacher from Ehden, a village in the north of Lebanon not far from Bsharri, and her mother was Palestinian. May grew up in the Land of the Cedars and went to Antoura College, a school founded by the Lazarist Order. In 1908, her father left Lebanon and settled in Egypt, where he took over the editorship of the newspaper *al-Mahrousah*. Unusually talented and with a command of English, French and Arabic, she made a name for herself in journalism and literature. Although women in general were not appreciated in her milieu, Ziadeh soon established a reputation as a literary critic and published an anthology of French poems under the pseudonym 'Isis Copia'. Her book *Fleurs de rêve* (*Flowers of Dreams*) was published in 1911. A committed feminist, she transformed her apartment in Cairo into a literary salon and welcomed, every Tuesday evening, contemporary

---

1.   Her real name was Marie. In his letters, Gibran sometimes refers to her as May and sometimes as Marie.

intellectuals: Taha Hussein, Yacoub Sarrouf, Lutfi es-Sayed, Abbas Mahmoud al-Aqqad, Edgar Jallad, Ismail Sabri, Mustafah Sadek, Antoun Gemayel, and Waly al-din Yakan, and she soon became their muse.

In 1912, May discovered Gibran. When she read his article 'The Day of My Birth' in the newspaper, she fell under the spell of the writer's style. That same year *Broken Wings* was published. May read the book, loved it, and wrote to Gibran to congratulate him. 'I share your fundamental principle which hails the free woman. A woman must be as free as a man to choose her marriage partner according to her own preferences and her intuition. Her life cannot be conditioned by the mould that her neighbors and acquaintances choose.'

Gibran wrote back. It was the beginning of a correspondence in Arabic which would continue until Gibran's death. What did the two expatriates tell each other? At first, they exchanged compliments and talked about literature. But soon a complicity developed between them, which then evolved into love. Gibran started his first letters, which he composed with more care than those he wrote to Mary Haskell, with the greeting, 'To the distinguished and talented writer', but he ended up calling her 'my beloved'. He told her how he spent his days, about his childhood, his dreams and his nostalgia for the East. He sent her invitation cards to his exhibitions or readings, press clippings about his work, and postcards featuring the painters he cherished. Sometimes he sketched little drawings in the margin; some were funny, others symbolic. On 24 March 1913, during a tributary ceremony to the Lebanese writer Khalil Moutran, which was taking place in Cairo, he even asked her to represent him and to read a text on his behalf.

May had a sensitive and dreamy nature. When the World War I broke out and mail delivery was suspended, the young girl held on to the memory of her distant correspondent and rejected all her suitors.

In an article published in 1916 in her father's newspaper, she expressed her longing to be with the one whose face she cherished, he who was so dear to her, but from whom she was separated by thousands of miles. She imagined herself soaring over the ocean to meet him. One guesses that in her romantic universe, Gibran already held an important place.

Without ever having met, the two writers felt very close to each other, so close that Gibran considered there were 'invisible threads' binding his thoughts to hers, and his soul to hers, and he imagined that May's spirit, thanks to what he called the translucent element, was with him wherever he went. He even used the first person plural, as in hundreds of letters addressed to Mary Haskell, to prove his soul and May's were united despite the distance that separated them.

> You expressed your regret that you were unable to attend the artistic banquet, and your regret surprises me; indeed, as a matter of fact it astonishes me. Do you not remember that we were together at the exhibition? Have you forgotten the way we moved from picture to picture? ... Evidently, the translucent element within us acts and moves without our knowledge. It sails across the sky on the other side of the globe ... The translucent element in us is mysterious, May, and a multitude of its activities are unknown to us. Whether we come to recognize it or not, it remains our hope and our goal; our destiny and our perfection; it is our Selves in our divine state. I believe, therefore, that were you to exert your memory a little you would remember our visit to the exhibition – so why don't you?

And in yet another letter:

> You have been in my thoughts ever since I last wrote to you. I have spent long hours thinking about you, talking to you, endeavoring to discover your secrets, trying to unravel your

mysteries. Even so, it is still surprising to me that I should have felt the presence of your ethereal Self in my studio, observing my movements, conversing and arguing with me, voicing your opinions on what I do.

In June 1921, May sent him her photo, a photo that inspired him to draw her portrait in charcoal. He was delighted to find a woman with a full, round face, short brown hair parted in the middle, with almond-shaped eyes and thick eyebrows, a sensual mouth and full lips. In her looks there was something expressive and bright that electrified him. There was also something a bit masculine in her appearance, a latent hardness which, rather than detracting from her beauty, enhanced it. May was the incarnation of the Oriental woman. 'What a beautiful photo it is! How beautiful this young girl is, and how clearly intelligence is marked in her eyes!' He thought long and hard about this snapshot, which put a face to his ethereal love stemming from an innocent, epistolary relationship. This girl had everything he looked for in a woman. But she was far away. And he was not yet ready to give up his freedom and leave the USA. But what did it matter? Not crossing the bridge and not taking the leap ... this kind of spiritual and intellectual love suited him perfectly. But what about her? Did he consider the false hopes that his beautiful words bred in the heart of his penfriend?

In October 1923, Gibran found himself love-starved. Posy, Micheline, Charlotte and Gertrude were no longer there. Mary had distanced herself. No longer holding back, he wrote to May to declare unceremoniously, 'You live in me, and I in you; you know this and I know it too.' In December of the same year, he persisted.

At this hour you are with me; you are with me, May ... and I know that we are nearer God's throne on this night than any time in the past ... Of all people you are the nearest to my soul, and the nearest to my heart, and our souls and hearts have never quarreled ... I love my little one, but I do not know in my mind why I love her. It is sufficient that I love her in my soul and in my heart. It is sufficient for me to rest my head on her shoulder when I am sad, lonely and in solitude, or when I am happy, entranced and full of wonder. It is sufficient for me to walk by her side to the top of the mountain and to tell her now and then, 'You are my companion. You are my companion.'

May proved to be modest and reserved, and when certain topics broached by her penfriend ruffled her feathers, either because he was being too audacious or because he criticised the formal tone which she adopted without realising it, she would sulk and retreat into a silence that would sometimes last for several months. She revealed her real feelings in her articles. In addition to the glowing reviews she made sure to devote to Gibran's work, she wrote several texts implicitly addressed to her beloved. In an article entitled, 'You, the Stranger', she expressed all the passion she held for 'he who knew not that she loved him' and 'whose voice she looked for among all the voices she heard'. But she was in doubt and wondered if she was deluding herself, if her love was imaginary. In 'At the Crossroads', she questions the man who inhabits her thoughts, 'Who are you? Are you a revelation spilling out of my poetry, a specter among the ghosts of my desire and my suffering? Or are you a tangible reality that crossed over the horizon of my life like a vessel crosses the sea to reach the distant shores?'

In a letter dated 15 January 1924, May became impatient and finally dared to declare her feelings to her penfriend. After a long introduction written in a playful tone, she reproached Gibran for having forgotten to send her holiday greetings. In it she invoked the longstanding rivalry between their two villages, Bsharri and Ehden.

She confessed her love to the one she nicknamed 'Al-Moustapha', the chosen one, like the central character in *The Prophet*:

> Gibran, I write these pages just to avoid telling you that you are my beloved, to avoid the word 'love'. I expect a lot from love, and I am worried that it will not give me everything I expect it to. I say this knowing that a little bit of love means a lot. But a little bit of love is not enough for me ... My outpourings to you – what do they mean? I do not really know what I mean by all this. But I know that you are my beloved and that I revere love ... How do I dare confess these thoughts to you? ... Thank God that I am writing all this down and not speaking it, because if you were here in the flesh now I would shrink back and keep away from you for a long while, and I would not allow you to see me again until you had forgotten my words. The sun has sunk below the distant horizon, and out of the strange clouds, wondrous in shape and form, there has appeared a single brilliant star, Venus, the Goddess of Love. I wonder whether this star is also inhabited by people like us, who love and are filled with longing. Might it not be possible that Venus is like me and has her own Gibran – a distant and beautiful presence who is in reality very near?

And what does Gibran reply to that? In his letter dated 26 February 1924, he starts by mentioning his love for storms, throws out a witticism about his beard, 'an event of international importance', and then declares to his penfriend:

> You tell me that you fear love; why, my little one? Do you fear the light of the sun? Do you fear the ebb and flow of the sea? ... I wonder why you fear love ... I know that a mean-spirited love does not please you, just as I know a mean-spirited love does not please me. You and I are never satisfied with what is parsimonious in spirit. We want a great deal. We want everything. We want perfection ... I say, Marie, do not be

apprehensive about love; do not be afraid, friend of my heart. We must surrender to it in spite of what it may bring in the way of pain, of desolation, of longing, and in spite of all the perplexity and bewilderment ... And now, come nearer. Bring your sweet forehead closer to me – like this, like this, and may God bless you and protect you, my heart's beloved companion.

Gibran's letter did not live up to May's expectations. True, he spoke of love. But his comments were so idealistic that they seemed impersonal and out of kilter with her own. Caught unawares by her unexpected attitude, Gibran decided to beat a retreat in order to safeguard his freedom or to save time. He knew his time was limited and probably preferred not to get involved in a relationship which would have demanded, from him as well as from his loved one, great sacrifices. May bitterly realised that there was a basic misunderstanding between her own desire and the ideal that Gibran had made of their relationship. She was sorry to have been so bold, so frank. For eight months, she remained incommunicative, a silence which Gibran found 'as long as eternity'.

In spite of all this, their correspondence resumed, albeit less frequently, until Gibran's death. The last letter she received from him included a drawing of a blue flame held in an open palm ... What a symbol! On learning of the artist's death, May let out a terrible cry of pain. Ten years later, she died, never having loved any other man.

❧⬥❧

Much ink has been spilled over the epistolary relationship between Gibran and May. Certain authors, exaggerating its importance in his life, claimed that he asked her to marry him. Others attribute her state of madness in her later days to Gibran's premature death, basing their claims on a photo of Gibran on which May scribbled, 'This here has been my tragedy for many years'. Both these theories are debatable. The letters available to us now (many were missing or scattered) do not mention marriage. Furthermore, the depression May suffered must also have been due to her sadness and solitude following the death of her parents and her best friend, Yacoub Sarrouf. She was also plagued by her relatives, who were trying to take control of her assets. Whatever the truth, the correspondence between the two writers remains one of the most prolific and most beautiful in Arabic literature, and is an excellent testimony to the formidable propensity Gibran had for loving, even without ever being able to possess, at a distance.

> They tell me, May, that I love people, and some reproach me for loving everybody. Yes, I love all people. I love them entirely without discrimination or preference ... But every heart has its special object of adoration, every heart has a special direction towards which it turns when it is all alone. Every heart has a hermitage to which it retires by itself to seek comfort and consolation. Every heart yearns for another heart with which it may join in order to enjoy life's blessings and peace or forget life's pain.

Admirable words from a man who never forgot to love, without ever having found the love of his life.

TEN

World War I

*T*he war in Europe spread like wildfire. Although Gibran was thousands of kilometres away from the battlefield, he was not immune to the tragedy; he found the news from Lebanon deeply distressing. Using the Allies' embargo as a pretext, the Ottoman authorities appropriated all the country's natural resources and were no longer ensuring fresh supplies to Beirut. Livestock was requisitioned. Hunting was prohibited. Epidemics and the invasion of locusts ravaging the harvests aggravated the situation. Famine was rampant. Skeletal children with bloated stomachs roamed the streets. The daily death toll in Beirut reached 100. In despair, the starving sold their goods for just a *ratl* (2.5 kg) of flour. In Aley, the martial court of the Ottoman military commander, Jamal Pacha, was not short of work. Opponents of the Ottoman occupation were reduced to silence by hanging in a public square. In 1915 and 1916, the Turks accused several Lebanese and Arab nationalists of high treason because of their contacts with the Allies, and sent them to the gallows. For Gibran, what was happening in Mount Lebanon was simply a replay of the tragedy that had taken place in Armenia. He felt guilty – guilty about being far from those who were 'dying in silence'. He knew that 'lamentations would not appease their hunger and that tears would not quench their thirst', so when he was assigned the post of Secretary of the Committee of Aid to the victims of Syria and Mount Lebanon, of which Amin Rihani was vice-president, he accepted unflinchingly. He wrote to Mary, 'It is a great responsibility, but I must shoulder it. Great tragedies enlarge the heart. I have never been given the chance to serve my people in a work of this sort. I am glad I can serve a little and I feel that God will help me.' He mustered up all his energy and solicited contributions from the Syrio-Lebanese communities in Boston and New York, and with the support of the American Red Cross, managed to send his stricken countrymen a shipload of food. In 1917, the day after the USA entered the war, Gibran became even more involved. He joined the Committee of Volunteers of Syria and Mount Lebanon, presided over by Ayub Tabet, his old classmate, and was placed in charge of recruiting Syrians and Lebanese from America who were ready to fight with the Allies to liberate the region from Ottoman rule. In September there were approximately 15,000 volunteers who joined the ranks of the Legion of the Orient in the French army based in Cyprus.

Basing their opinions on Gibran's 'political' activities during this period, some essayists have made him into a doctrinarian, an ideologist, a champion of the Syrian cause. They were far off the mark, however. Gibran was by no means a politician. 'Spare me the political events and power struggles, as the whole earth is my homeland and all men are my fellow countrymen,' he wrote in *A Tear and a Smile*. To those who insisted on politically labelling him, he said, 'I am not a politician, nor do I wish to become one.' Furthermore, in *The Tempests*, which tells the story of Yusuf Fakhry, who at the age of thirty decided to retire from the tumult of society and settle in a hermitage far from the city, Gibran has his hero say, 'I ran away from the politicians who were seeking power and in the process destroying their people by throwing gold dust in their eyes and filling their ears with empty talk.' Gibran's sense of responsibility, though, did prompt him to get involved when duty called. He was primarily a reformer preoccupied with the human condition, which he wanted to liberate from all forms of slavery, and he relentlessly advocated his ideal of freedom. In doing so, he called for the liberation of all Arab territories occupied by the Ottomans.

Absorbed in his humanitarian activity and shattered by the tragic news coming from Europe and the Levant, Gibran slowed down his literary output. He did publish *A Tear and a Smile* in 1914, but this anthology was merely a collection of Arabic articles which had previously appeared in *al-Mohajer* and which he himself was reluctant to have published. 'It was about a past period in my life which was lived in lamentation and lyricism.' The fifty-six articles are inspired by a humanistic outlook and contain reflections on life, love and the situation in Lebanon and Syria. Gibran was certainly one of the pioneers of poetic prose, a literary form that was still a novelty in Arabic literature.

It was around this time that Gibran, undoubtedly egged on by Mary Haskell, found the need, or at least the desire, to express himself in English, the language which would open many doors for him and would allow him to reach American audiences. He could sense that there was a wide field to explore. 'Westerners are weary of the phantoms of their souls and tired of themselves. They will hang on to anything exotic and extraordinary, especially if it comes from the East,' he wrote to May Ziadeh. In 1918 he added, 'People have undergone a big change over the course of the last three years. They are hungry for beauty, for truth, and for that which exists beyond beauty and truth.' If his command of English was not good enough, he was not about to let that become an obstacle. He plunged back into the works of Shakespeare, read and reread the King James version of the Bible.

Bit by bit, his willpower and long, hard work enabled him to adopt the language of Shakespeare without rejecting his own language, which remained alive within him. 'I continue to think in Arabic,' he confided to Mary Haskell. Barbara Young, who was his assistant in his later days, reports that often 'there was not an English word that conveyed with perfect exactitude the meaning of the thought he wanted to express, there, being, as he said, "fifty words in Arabic to give expression to the many aspects of love," while in English there is but one. His vast Arabic vocabulary made him feel cramped in his adopted tongue. However, that very fact resulted in the pure and almost perfect clarity and simplicity of his English style.' Gibran made rapid progress. He opted for an uncluttered structure and used the Bible as a model. 'Kahlil's English is the most refined I know; it is refined and marvelously simple,' Mary noted in her diary. She added, without exaggerating, 'He knows more English than any of us, for he is conscious of the bony structure of the language, its solar system. And he *creates* English.' In fact, Gibran had a boundless imagination and a sense of rhythm. 'Poets,' he says, 'must listen to the rhythm of the sea. You can find the same rhythm in the *Book of Job* and all the magnificent passages in the Old Testament. This is the music that should inspire us, as the rustling of the leaves in the wind.' His English is classical and he uses words like *aught, verily, yea*, yet his style is not stilted. It bends and flows to its 'maritime' music, its imagery and its allusions. It has the limpidity of parables.

Which book would he start with? There was, of course, *The Prophet*, which had been germinating since his childhood, but it was making very slow progress. He had to find a less daunting project, one that could encompass his ideas and his newly adopted language. Gibran wondered. Who, with all impunity, could denounce the stupidity and cowardice of men and expose society's veils and masks? A madman! The idea took hold of him. He could not forget Qoshaya, in the Sacred Valley, and the grotto where people thought they could cure madmen by chaining them to the rocks. In 'Youhanna the Madman' he had already stated that madmen were the ones who dared tell the truth, the ones who broke with obsolete traditions and were 'crucified' because they aspired to change. In the plays published posthumously, *The Blind* and *Lazarus and his Beloved*, the madman on stage is an enlightened narrator who comments philosophically on the story being played out before him. For Gibran, 'Madness is the first step towards unselfishness. Be mad and tell us what is behind the veil of "sanity". The purpose of life is to bring us closer to those secrets, and madness is the only means.' *The Madman* would be the title of his next book! Now all he had to do was to write it.

Meanwhile, he wrote for a new literary magazine, *The Seven Arts*, edited by a young American poet, James Oppenheim. This magazine, in which several famous writers like John Dos Passos, D. H. Lawrence and Bertrand Russell also wrote, proved to be the springboard of his career and gave him a name in various New York artistic circles. He published some of his drawings in it but mainly his first English writings, like *The Night and the Madman* or *The Supreme Mother*, revised and fine-tuned by the kind and conscientious Mary Haskell. His collaboration with the magazine, however, was short-lived. Because of its pacifist views and open criticism of the American involvement in the war, Gibran soon found himself obliged to resign from the editing committee so as not to be misjudged by his Syrian and Lebanese friends. 'I am against the war,' he explained, 'But it is for this reason that I am using this war ...'

And what of his visual art? 'The air is full of cries,' he wrote to Mary, 'and one cannot breathe without getting the taste of blood.' Gibran was stifled, but he refused to give in to despair. Wearing his white *abaya*, a wide garment which he always wore in his studio, he took refuge in painting. He finished, among others, a large canvas of a mother holding a child (him?) and surrounded by two daughters. Thanks to Alexander Morton, he was able to exhibit at the Montross Gallery at 550 Fifth Avenue, starting on 14 December 1914. The exhibition, his first since returning from Paris, received lukewarm reviews in the New York press, but he earned 5,000 dollars for it. In 1917 there were two other exhibitions, one at Knoedler & Co. in New York, where forty of his aquarelles were hanging next to the paintings of Bonnard, Carrière, Cézanne, and Picasso. The other was at Doll & Richards in Boston.

On the evening of the exhibition at Montross, Gibran and Mary found themselves alone in his apartment. To his astonishment, she started undressing. Encouraged and delighted, he approached her, put his hands on her body, but then decided to desist. In a moment of sudden realisation, he thought better of pursuing any physical relationship. Their spiritual connection had reached such a dimension that he was worried it would become tarnished by a sexual encounter, which would invariably complicate matters between them.

The years 1914 to 1916 were full of new encounters. Gibran could often be seen in the fashionable circles of New York high society, in the company of influential women. He met Rose O'Neill, the successful artist who did his portrait, Thomas Raymond, the mayor of New York, and Amy Lowell, the American poet.

He also met Albert Ryder, the famous symbolist painter. Ryder lived in poverty in an insufficiently heated room in a dilapidated building. He slept on the floor or on three chairs placed together in a row and drank like a fish in an effort to eradicate the memory of the woman who had left him. The two men took a liking to each other. Gibran did his portrait and added it to his 'Temple of Art', to which he had recently added Percy MacKaye, the playwright, and Ruth Saint Denis, the dancer. Denis's graceful movements inspired him in more than one drawing and she was undoubtedly the muse for the parable of *The Wanderer*, where his character says, 'The soul of a philosopher stays inside his head; the soul of the poet is found in his heart; the soul of a dancer lives entirely in her body.' It was during this phase that Gibran was invited several times to the Poetry Society of America, which included among its founding members Corinne Roosevelt Robinson, sister of the future American president, Franklin Delano Roosevelt. He chose extracts from *The Madman*, which he was in the process of writing, and read them to an attentive audience.

In the autumn of 1916, Gibran made himself a new friend, a man who would later write a biography of him that was considered rather controversial because it was too personal and fictionalised. This man, well known to the Lebanese, was none other than the writer Mikhail Naimy, who lived to be a centenarian. Originally from a high mountain village often entrenched in fog, Baskinta, Naimy attended a seminary in Russia before going to the United States to study law and literature. What did these two men have in common, other than their national background? Both wrote in the magazine *al-Founoun*, both believed in reincarnation and both struggled for the liberation of their country. In the Committee of Volunteers, Gibran was appointed secretary for correspondence in English, and Naimy in Arabic. Was anything more needed to seal their friendship? But the war would soon separate the new accomplices. Mikhail Naimy, alias 'Mischa', was sent to the French front with the American Military Corps. He found himself in Bordeaux, then in the Argonne woods. Even once he had returned to New York and was safe and sound, he never forgot the painful experience of the trenches.

In December 1916, Gibran met Rabindranath Tagore, the famous Indian poet and winner of the 1913 Nobel Prize for Literature. 'He is beautiful to look at and to be with, but I was disappointed with his voice. It is bodyless, and it made his poems less real to me,' he wrote to Mary. Three years later, a New York journalist drew a parallel between these two men by pointing out that both used parables in their writing, both commanded the English language as well as their own, and both were talented in not only poetry but also other domains of art.

At the end of 1916, Mary sent Gibran a small piece of a meteorite from Arizona. Passionate about astronomy, either because it brought him closer to God or because it helped him demonstrate the mechanisms of the universe, he was overjoyed to receive it. 'The meteorite, the precious meteorite is the most wonderful thing I have ever had. It feeds my imagination and it sends my thoughts into space and makes the infinite nearer and less strange to my soul.'

With the end of the war imminent, Gibran focused on his writing. In August, he wrote a story in Arabic entitled 'Satan', where he imagines a meeting between a North Lebanese priest named Semaan and a dying devil. 'I build convents and monasteries on the foundations of fear,' claims Satan. 'I build stalls of wine and houses of debauchery on the foundations of luxury. If I stopped existing, pleasure and fear would be abolished in this world, and with their disappearance, desires and hopes would stop existing in the human heart. Life would become empty and cold, like a harp with broken strings. I am the eternal Satan.' Worried about losing his privileges, Father Semaan decides to save the devil. 'You must live because if you die and people find out about it, they will no longer be afraid of hell, they will stop praying, and they will wallow in sin. I will sacrifice my hatred of you on the altar of my love for man,' he declared to clear his conscience. The text, where irony and cynicism intertwine, is a condemnation of the clergy, whose power is based on the fear of Evil that is engrained in the faithful. The author portrays Satan as an invention by men to label 'the strange power that directs the storms towards our houses and brings the plague upon us'. It is not a far cry from Herman Melville's

The Merchant of Lightning Poles, in which the narrator converses with a travelling salesman who barters with men's fears.

Gibran himself returns to this idea in a manifesto entitled 'The New Frontier',[1] in which he questions his brothers:

> Are you a religious leader who weaves a robe for his body with the candor of the people, fashioning a crown for his head with the simplicity of their hearts and pretends to hate Satan so he can live off his benefits? Or are you a devout and pious man who sees a foundation for the progress of the nation in the virtue of the individual and a ladder towards the Universal Spirit in the quest for secrets of the soul? If you are the first one, you are a heretic, impious, even if you fast during the day and pray at night. If you are the second, you are a white lily in the garden of the truth.

Under the vigilant eye of Mary Haskell, he wrote new passages for the future book *The Prophet*, under the working title of *Counsels*. It was beginning to take shape, and in the meantime he finished *The Madman*, which consisted of thirty-four parables and poems, comparable to the tales of the Sufi poet Farid Uddin Attar.[2] But where was he going to publish this first book in English? He sent the manuscript to three editors, all of whom refused to publish it on the grounds that it was literature 'that doesn't sell'. But Fate intervened. During a banquet organised on the occasion of the publication of *The Book of Self* by Oppenheim by a new publishing company founded by Alfred A. Knopf, Gibran managed to get an appointment with the latter, thanks to the recommendations of the poet Witter Bynner and the French ambassador to Washington, Pierre de Lanux, whose

---

1. Published in the Egyptian newspaper *al-Hilal* on 1 April 1923, this text is reprinted in *Wonders and Curiosities*.
2. See 'Solomon and the Ant in Love' or 'The Woman and the Dog' in Farid Uddin Attar, *The Divine Book*, Albin Michel, 1961, pp. 92 and 426. See also Attar, *The Book of Secrets*, Two Oceans, 1985, and *The Book of Proof*, Fayard, 1981.

portrait Gibran had done. Gibran was charmed by Knopf, who agreed to publish him. 'The more I see Alfred Knopf, the more I like him. He is not a philanthropist. He is honest. He leaves nothing to chance.'

Who was this character that gave Gibran his head start? Alfred Abraham Knopf was born in New York on 12 September 1892. In 1908, at Columbia University, he became impassioned about history and literature. On returning from a trip to Europe, he determined to become a publisher rather than a lawyer, as his family would have preferred. However, it was not easy for an inexperienced young man to penetrate the closed world of publishing. In October 1912, he was hired as an accountant at Doubleday & Co., where he learned the tricks of the trade. In 1915, with the financial assistance of his father, who later joined the firm, and the cooperation of his fiancée, Blanche Wolf, who then became his wife, he founded his own publishing house, right in the middle of New York City, and called it 'Alfred A. Knopf, Inc.'. Alfred Knopf soon became the publisher of some of the greatest foreign writers: Thomas Mann, Jorge Amado, Jules Romain, André Gide, Paul Morand, Albert Camus, Jean-Paul Sartre, Yasunari Kawabata and Gabriel García Márquez. Placing himself at the forefront of American and British literature, he published D. H. Lawrence, Witter Bynner, Katherine Mansfield, Robert Graves and Ezra Pound, who recommended his publishing house to their colleagues.

Knopf founded 'The Book Table', an association of publishers, booksellers, librarians and other literary men. Being interested in the artistic aspect of book designing and publishing, he later also became a member of several book arts groups. In 1950, Alfred A. Knopf was commended for having given his books style and elegance by the American Institute of Graphic Arts. No one summarised his character better than Thomas Mann, who was quoted by *The Washington Post*

(12 August 1984) to have said of him, 'He is a mixture of business sense and strategic friendship with the spirit!'

The relationship between Knopf and Gibran went through several stages. Their unpublished correspondence, as evidenced in Knopf's letters to Gibran on 25 February and 19 March 1926, shows us that Knopf was very mindful of the cost of the books he published and uncompromising as to the royalties. Alfred Knopf greatly appreciated his wife, Blanche, who became a major figure in the firm. He is quoted as having said about her, 'She brought charm, sophistication, and enlightenment to a publishing world predominantly masculine. She has a special place in the publishers "Hall of Fame".' As for the letters Gibran wrote to Blanche Knopf, they are interesting in more ways than one. In one of them, Gibran informs her that he was born on 6 January (and not 6 December) 1883, thereby putting an end to a longstanding controversy as to the accuracy of this date of birth. In the autumn of 1925, she asked Gibran, for advertising purposes, for permission to exploit the fact that *The Prophet* had been translated into Hebrew by Isaac Horowitz. He said he preferred to wait until it was actually published before making an issue of the translation. Gibran's relationship with his editor would soon become more informal. She invited him over for tea at her place and they started calling each other 'Blanche' and 'Kahlil'. Blanche was the sociable one with the 'human touch' at the firm. From the time she was named vice-president in 1921, she played a key role in scouting out authors and translators when she travelled to Europe and South America, thereby establishing the firm's reputation abroad and cementing personal friendships with noteworthy authors.

In mid-October 1918, *The Madman*, including three of the author's illustrations, was finally published, and it was dedicated, as to be expected, to MEH. To encourage sales, the editor distributed a pamphlet stating, 'It is not surprising that Rodin has high hopes for this Arab poet. In his parables and poems he seems, in a curious way, to express in English what Rodin was able to express in marble and clay. Rodin has compared Gibran to William Blake.' Having attributed these words to the sculptor would have been risky had the eminent sculptor still been alive. But he was not around to deny ever having said them; he had passed away in November 1917, and Gibran insisted on paying tribute to his memory in a poem entitled 'Master of Clay'.

The Madman, of which certain texts were initially written in Arabic and then translated into English by the author himself and his protectress, tells the story of a sensitive but 'different' character and begins with how he became mad. 'In my folly,' he observes, 'I found freedom and salvation at the same time.' He senses he has divine essence; he makes contact with God and talks to Him. In uniting himself with God and nature, he consolidates his internal cohesion. But in the process, he does not forget about men. He does not want to break the links that unite the visible to the invisible. He observes the world with new eyes, ironic and mocking the blindness of justice, human foolishness and the vanity of philosophical discussions. The style of the ensemble is sober, the English language lending itself marvellously to conciseness. The tone bitter and sarcastic, *The Madman* is a turning point in Gibran's writing career, not only because it was his first book in English but also because the violence and the rancour that characterised his first writings give way here to contemplation and spiritual elevation. Although the work sometimes seems incoherent, illustrated by the juxtaposition of a timely text called 'Defeat' (written after the defeat of Serbia in 1918) with pieces written specifically for inclusion in the book, a critic of the times, Marguerite Wilkinson, elegises it. 'Kahlil Gibran is writing poems and parables that have an individual music, a naïve charm and distinction and a structural symmetry based on symbol, contrast, repetition and parallelism.'

Gibran sent a copy of the book to May Ziadeh, who found it grim and cruel. Accustomed to the eulogies of his penfriend, he answered her in adapting a verse from the Bible: 'What is the merit of a man to have the approval of the whole world if he loses that of Marie?' He also sent a copy to Gertrude Barrie, his secret lover. The reason that Gibran continued to hide this affair was undoubtedly so as not to hurt Mary, who would have found it difficult to accept that another woman was able to get from him what she was denied; also because this relationship, which had nothing platonic about it, contradicted his status as 'prophet'.

If the truth be told, Gibran had an unverifiable number of relationships on the sly, platonic or carnal: Gertrude Stern, whom he met in 1930 and who considered herself his last love; Marie Qahwaji; Marie El-Khoury, a jeweller, who from 1922 often welcomed him in her home, Madeline Mason-Manheim, his translator[1]; and many others besides. Helena Ghostine, like Micheline and Charlotte, claims that Gibran was 'a lady's man' and tells a juicy anecdote which is quite revealing about the writer's behaviour: 'One day, Gibran asked me to buy him an umbrella. "I want to give it to Mariana," he assured me. I went all around the shops to find a very original one, one that could easily be distinguished in a crowd. Several weeks later, I saw this same umbrella in the hands of a woman I did not know. I pretended to take a great interest in the object and asked her where she had bought it. Blushing, she answered that her Lebanese friend had given it to her.'

Gibran lived these adventures clandestinely, either to safeguard the reputation of the ladies with whom he was involved, or to live up

---

1.   See al-Hawadess, January 12, 1979. In 1926, Madeline Mason-Manheim (1908-1990) translated *The Prophet* into French. A year ago, Gibran illustrated her book *Hill Fragments*, published by Brentano's with a preface by Arthur Symons.

to the image he wanted to give himself: that of an ascetic detached from earthly contingencies, that of a superior being who 'took love in the spirit and not in the body'. It is only in *Sand and Foam*, which came out several years later, that he finally conceded that 'even the most winged spirit cannot escape from the desires of life'.

In November 1918, the Armistice was finally declared. With overflowing enthusiasm, Gibran wrote to Mary, who had closed her school to direct Cambridge School, 'It is the most sacred day since the birth of Jesus!'

ELEVEN

From Nature toward the Infinite

*I*n May 1919, Gibran's sixth book in Arabic, *The Processions,* was published by the magazine *Mir'at al Gharb* ('The Mirror of the West') with eight of his drawings and an introduction by the editor-in-chief, Naseeb Arida. It consists of a philosophical dialogue written in the form of a 203-verse poem. One speaker is the voice of a cynic disenchanted with the world and critical of the artificial values of civilisation; the other is more optimistic, more serene, chanting a hymn to nature and the uniqueness of existence, represented by the *nay.* This instrument was invariably used by the Sufis, who reveal the hidden secrets of the 'Most Sublime', and it symbolises the soul that aspires to return to the divine source from which it was separated. Gibran explained to Mary that *The Processions* represents the aspects of life as seen by a person with double vision – a city-loving self and a spontaneous and ingenious other, like the young shepherds of the Middle East. The second accepts and chants the song of life in harmony with itself without analysing or doubting, or debating or defining. As in *The Madman*, the author makes a clean break with the ideas advocated in his previous Arabic books. *The Processions* is an invitation to contemplation. Its simple, sincere and spontaneous language, free from all archaic expressions without being outright modern (the poem is composed in two meters of the prosodic classical Arabic), elicited strong reactions from purist critics like al-Aqaad and Omar Farroukh. But nothing could stop Gibran's determination to break the barriers. Both on the stylistic and ideological planes, he preferred anarchy to respect for conventions. The word 'tradition' was anathema to him. He gave free reign to his unbridled imagination without attaching much importance to the constraints of the prosody or the stringent rules governing Arabic which he often came to ignore in his writing.

At the end of 1919, Knopf published a collection of Gibran's pictures entitled *Twenty Drawings*. For the preface, the editor used a text by the art critic, Alice Raphael Eckstein. Previously published in *The Seven Arts* in March 1917, the text claimed that the work of Gibran was at the 'frontier of the East and the West, of symbolism and idealism'. She was won over by the artist's style. He painted in much the same way that he wrote, and he wrote visually, as if he was painting. How could he possibly give up painting, which had been such an intrinsic part of him ever since he was a child? Why abandon writing, which allowed him to express his ideas in Arabic, and more recently in English too? Gibran had carried on his painting and writing careers without ever disassociating one from the other. 'I spend my life writing and drawing, and the pleasure that these two arts bring me surpasses all other pleasure,' he claimed. 'The fire that fuels my feelings consumes ink and paper.' For him, the visual world and the literary world merge, thereby becoming indistinguishable. One can easily say that Gibran paints with words, and his painting appears like the physical expression of his ideas. It reflects his metaphysical angst and always conveys a message. Attuned to the human condition, he represents only characters – real or imaginary – and shows a great predilection for the nude, which constitutes, as he often claimed, 'the most accurate and most beautiful symbol of life'.

Through Fred Holland Day, Gibran discovered symbolism and was so enraptured by his mentor that one sees disturbing connections between Day's photographs and his student's works. Day's photos entitled *Archer in the Woods* or *Youth in Rocky Landscape* heralded the Gibranian universe. The same is true for the photos entitled *Nude Youth with Lyre* and *Orpheus*, both very similar to Gibran's *Orpheus*. Furthermore, there is a striking resemblance between the character figuring in Day's *The Storm God* and the central figure in Gibran's *The Storm*, even down to their postures.

If truth be told, Gibran's skill in painting was self-taught, albeit that in Paris he attended the Académie Julian and the Marcel-Béronneau Studio briefly. In terms of images, one author has pointed out that 'Gibran did not follow an academic or methodical learning program and never received a diploma of any kind. Just like a bird, he pecked wherever he saw fit and then rose towards the peak of his spiritual dream world.'[1]

Early on, however, even before his apprenticeship in France, Gibran instinctively opted for a particular style: between his first drawings sketched in Lebanon and his last paintings, there exists a certain similarity, a continuity. Unlike many famous painters, Gibran had, from the outset, drawn himself a precise path that he forced himself to follow scrupulously – all the while improving his style. As early as 1908, at a dinner at Mary Haskell's, he had defined his vision of art.

> Some people think the business of art to be a mere imitation
> of nature. But Nature is far too sublime and too subtle to
> be successfully imitated. No artist can ever reproduce even

---

1. Cf. Boulos Tawk, *The Personality of Gibran in its Constitutional and Existential Dimensions*, vol. II, 1984, p. 239.

the least of Nature's creations and miracles. Besides, what is the point of imitating Nature when she is so open and so accessible to all those who can see and hear? The purpose of art is rather to understand Nature and to reveal her meaning. It is to convey the soul of a tree rather than to produce a fruitful likeness of the tree by drawing its trunk and branches. It is to reveal the conscience of the sea, not to portray so many foaming waves or so much blue water. The mission of art is to bring out the unfamiliar from the most familiar, from nature to the infinite.

Impervious to the artistic trends of his day, cubism and surrealism, Gibran preferred to evolve along the fringe of the pioneers. He latched on to the symbolism of William Blake who, no doubt, left a profound impact on him. Gibran's library, conserved in Bsharri, contains Blake's *The Marriage of Heaven and Earth* and at least four books on Blake, among which are Lawrence Binyon's *The Drawings and Engravings of William Blake* and Elizabeth Luther's *The Art of William Blake*, a present from Mary Haskell. His correspondence often alludes to the great British artist's work as evidenced in a letter to Mary dated 6 October 1915, 'Blake is the god-man. His drawings are so far the profoundest things done in English – and his vision, putting aside his drawings and his poems is the most godly.' From Gibran's first exhibition at Harcourt Studios in 1904, the critic of the *Evening Transcript* reveals that one of the exhibited paintings 'calls to mind one of the mystical masterpieces of William Blake'. Gibran would have us believe that Rodin called him 'the Blake of the twentieth century'. Mary Haskell once wrote to Gibran, 'Blake is mighty. The voice of God and the finger of God are in what he does. He really feels closer to you, Kahlil, than all the rest.' She was right to say so. For Gibran, Blake was more than just one of several sources of inspiration: Jean Delville, Odilon Redon, Pierre Puvis de Chavannes – whose murals adorned the Boston Public Library and whose simplicity and purity Gibran admired – Fernand Khnopff, Aubrey Beardsley, Edward Burne-Jones and the Pre-Raphaelites. Blake was his true spiritual father, his guiding light. Wherever you look in *Pity, Whirlwind of Lovers* or *The House of Death*, you find winged women, petrified creatures, contorted bodies, nude figures, and piles of cadavers inhabiting the pictorial world of Gibran. Blake's *Queen Catherine's Dream* (1825) calls to mind Gibran's drawings, with his evanescent women, ethereal, with open hands, draped in togas.

Gibran identified with Blake's expressionistic symbolism, his rejection of slavish imitation of nature, his dreamlike fascination, the mythical content and almost mystical quality of his art, and his vision of a lost union to be regained. Like Blake, Gibran also considered these elements as an invitation for man to open his heart to the bliss of the divine that he holds within, that is, his spirit of rebellion. On the other hand, Gibran's world is more serene, hence less violent and less susceptible to the notions of hell, the destructive forces of Evil and the apocalypse, all of which obsessed the author of *The Marriage of Heaven and Hell*. Another point of contrast is that for Gibran, the imminence of the divine revealed itself and found fulfilment in nature, and not in the creative imagination he called 'poetic genius' although Gibran did not fail to appreciate it. Because if, for Blake, 'Where man is not, nature is barren,' nature, for the author of *The Prophet*, is the door to the Infinite. In terms of technique, Gibran, like his muse, rarely drew the human form from a model, yet he knew how to represent it accurately, thanks to his keen sense of observation and the power of his visual imagination. This ability would explain how he was able to achieve the portraits of Posy and Sultana. Gibran memorised their facial traits and saw mentally, very clearly, what he wanted to draw.

Gibran's work was also greatly influenced by Eugene Carrière, whom Gibran considered the artist closest to his heart. Enchanted by the haziness predominating in the paintings of the Frenchman, Gibran was inspired by many of his portraits as well as by his other paintings. It is a stunning coincidence that they both painted the portrait of the pamphleteer, Henri Rochefort. Between Gibran's *The Murmur of Silence* and Carrière's *The Death of Gauguin*, there is a definite similarity. Carrière's famous compositions dedicated to motherhood, in particular *Two Intertwining Bodies* and *Mother and Child*, are reminiscent of Gibran's paintings and drawings between 1908 and 1918, among which is also a painting entitled *Mother and Child*. 'One single medium, one single light, is what the river going towards the sea teaches the artist ... the limitlessness of the horizon, the boundlessness of the universe ... a single humanity, a single reason come together to establish equilibrium in the world. All the aspects of humanity are bound to come together in the law of harmony.' This idea of Carrière's was intended to instil the feeling of union in man, and Gibran adhered to this belief totally.

If Gibran's work is illustrated by a certain continuity, it is no less true that it went through several stages. It is difficult to define them, however, as none of the paintings left behind were signed or included a title or a date, and there was never a precise inventory taken of them.

The first phase (1896–1904) corresponds to the initial phase of the artist and comprises drawings in pencil or ink, heralds of future works, some of which ended up illustrating the collection of poems published by Day and his friends. From this period we find, for example, a sketch representing a winged man lying on his back in the middle of a poppy field. The figure calls to mind the woman lying down in Blake's *Pity* and other drawings, which already abounded with mystical symbolism.

Between 1908 and 1910, in Paris, Gibran dabbled in oil painting and completed pieces such as the well-known *Autumn*, exhibited in the Salon du Printemps in 1910 at the Grand Palais. He excelled in

Kahlil Gibran, as photographed by Fred Holland Day (1897)

Left to right: Kamila, Sultana and
Mariana, as photographed by
Fred Holland Day (1901)

Bsharri, 1912 (Collection
Ghazi Geagea)

Fred Holland Day,
as photographed by
Frederick H. Evans
in England

Portrait of May Ziadeh
by Gibran, charcoal, 1920–1
(Gibran Museum)

The priest Yusuf Haddad, Gibran's
teacher at Al-Hikma College
(portrait by César Gemayel)

Yusuf Huwayyik, Gibran's friend

Josephine Preston Peabody ('Posy')
in 1892

Emilie Michel ('Micheline'), by Gibran
(Telfair Museum of Art, Savannah)

Naimy and Gibran
at Cahoonzie

Mary Haskell in 1926 (painting by Willem Adriaan van Konijnenburg, Telfair Museum of Art, Savannah)

Charlotte Teller

Kahlil Gibran (front row, second from left) in the studio of Marcel-Béronneau in Paris (1909)

A letter in Arabic from Gibran to
Helena Ghostine

Gibran's friend, Helena Ghostine

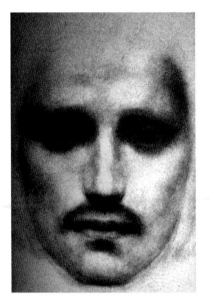

Face of al-Mustafa, frontispiece for
The Prophet, charcoal, 1923
(Gibran Museum)

Gibran in his room in front of a tapestry
representing Christ

Autumn, oil on canvas by Gibran
(1909), exhibited in Paris in 1910
(Gibran Museum)

The Three Stages of Being, illustration
for *The Prophet*, watercolour, 1923
(Gibran Museum)

Members of the Pen League, September 1920. From left to right: Naseeb Arida,
Gibran, Abdul Massih Haddad, Mikhail Naimy

One of the last photographs of Gibran

portrait art and completed a series of charcoal drawings of the artists of his day. The sketches, with thin sideways hatchings, sweet faces with vaguely defined hairlines and without details, eyes half closed, and bodies leaning over or turning three-quarters to the right, call to mind the studies of Leonardo da Vinci, the famous *Woman's Head* in particular. Also, the inclusion of several portraits in the same painting, like *The Blind, Four Faces*, or even *Three Faces Mounted by Flying Faces and an Angel*, occurs frequently in the drawings of Da Vinci, who obviously had a great impact on the work of Gibran.

Between 1910 and 1914, a new period saw more clarity and mastery in his work. Gibran painted in oil or drew charcoal works which featured recurring symbolic images, inhabited by centaurs, asexual characters, androgens, sometimes hermaphrodites, transfixed in meditative postures, shrivelled up or huddled together, intertwined, crucified, in the midst of a setting that evokes the world at the dawn of earthly paradise. In certain paintings, the influence of Rembrandt is noticeable: the dark background and highly illuminated hands and faces. In December 1914, after his exhibition at the Montross Gallery, he declared, 'My entire being is directed towards a new beginning steeped in freshness. This exhibition is the end of a chapter in my life.'

Between 1914 and 1920, Gibran tried the wash technique of drawing without changing anything basic in his work. The characters became more ethereal, more transparent, but the forms were less precise and the contours too blurred. The figures were sketched and shadowed in pencil. This technique in itself has too much chromatic vagueness and was less successful than his oil paintings. From this period we have a series of paintings on the theme of motherhood, a theme already dealt with, albeit differently, during the earlier phases.

In 1920, Gibran says that 'one phase has ended and another has started.' Between 1920 and 1923, his aquarelles are carefully detailed.

The colours have identity and clarity. The drawings in lead pencil on paper, *The Slave* and *The Divine World*, are characterised by harmonious composition. It is during this period that he exhibited at the Women's City Club in Boston, where he finished drawings that would later illustrate the text of *The Prophet*.

The last phase covers the period from 1923 to 1931, the year of his death. It brings together the most sombre canvases, where characters fade, ceding their place to phantom-like silhouettes. One can feel the anguish clutching at the artist. Was this new? In every example of Gibran's visual work reigns a great sadness, although hope is never totally absent. Lowered heads, crushed figures, grief-stricken mothers ... Should one attribute this melancholy to the romantic lyricism he inherited from Day? From her first meeting with Gibran, Posy reproached him for always looking sad. This temperament, exacerbated by his exile and the deaths in his family, find an explanation in one passage in *Broken Wings*: 'The life of someone who was not conceived by melancholy and who never experienced the contractions of despair is like a blank page in the book of existence.'

Taking all of this into account, one question remains: was Gibran a great painter? Some people claim that Gibran did not create anything new, that he was not an innovator, that he did not fit into the scheme of modernism, that he often repeated himself, and that in the long run, his procession of nude bodies with theatrical gestures end up being boring. Others critique his technique, his construction of tableaux. In fact, as with Blake, the visual work of Gibran is intimately linked to his writings; and if many of his paintings illustrate his books, it is undoubtedly to link more closely the word and the image. It is not possible to judge the painting of Gibran as separate from his thinking and his writings. It is part of a whole. Is it not an insult to someone who calls for the unity of all creation to contest the unity of his visual and verbal world?

TWELVE

The Pen League

On the night of 20 April 1920, Abdul Massih Haddad, the editor of the magazine *As Sayeh*, called for a meeting of Lebanese and Syrian writers from New York at his house. In their discussion, they realised that they had to do something to 'lift Arabic literature out of the quagmire, that is to say, the stagnation and imitation in which it had embedded itself.' It needed new blood. They decided to establish a committee to modernise it and aimed at grouping the writers and unifying their efforts in the advancement of Arabic literature. Finding it an excellent idea, Gibran invited all the founding members to meet at his house the following week.

On 28 April, nine writers showed up at 51 West 10th Street, Gibran's studio. This group included eminent writers such as Amin Rihani, Mikhail Naimy, Wadih Bahout, Rashid Ayub, Elia Abu Madi, Naseeb Arida, Nadra Haddad, Elias Atallah and William Catzeflis. They named their committee *Ar-Rabita al-Qalamiiah* ('The Pen League') and defined its goals, two of which were to publish the works of its members and of other worthy Arab authors and to encourage the translation of masterpieces from world literature into Arabic.

Gibran was elected president, 'Mischa' (Mikhail Naimy) advisor, and Catzeflis treasurer. They chose a verse from the Hadith, the most significant Muslim text after the Koran, as their motto: 'How marvelous are the treasures hidden under the throne of Allah (God) that only the poets can reveal them.'

What became of this new organisation? Its members met fairly regularly from 1920 until the death of Gibran, the most active member, in 1931. They published a number of articles in *As Sayeh*, and once a year a special issue, like an anthology of their contributions, came out. Thanks to the iconoclastic and rebellious ideas it advocated, *Ar Rabita* ended up being the symbol of renaissance in Arabic literature.

For Gibran, the Arabic language had no future unless it was liberated from the old moulds and the 'slavery of the superficial, literary sentences'. He believed it was crucial to initiate a real dialogue with the West and to incorporate the influence of European culture, without being dominated by it, into his native language. 'The spirit of the West is a friend if we can take from it what we need but becomes an enemy if we have to accommodate it and bend ourselves to it.' It is creative thought, 'the will to go forward', which, in his eyes, guarantees the permanence of a language. In the absence of such creative thought, 'the future of the Arabic language' (the title of one of his articles) looks quite grim. 'If the creative energy wanes, the language stops evolving, for all lack of evolution implies regression, and regression implies death and decay.'

In August 1920, an anthology of thirty-one articles by Gibran, previously published in various Arabic papers, was published by *Al-Hilal* in Cairo. It was Emil Zaydan, the editor-in-chief, who took the initiative to publish this book, eloquently entitled *The Tempests*. Zaydan had come into contact with Gibran through May Ziadeh. In a letter to the one he called 'Emil Effendi', Gibran expressed as much concern over 'the body of the book as over its soul'. He had given his editor detailed instructions on formatting, font, page layout, etc. so that the work would appear well designed, a sign of respect he had for the book and his readers. The fixing of the price and copyright conditions he left up to the editor. This was proof enough that Gibran, to the dismay of his critics, was indifferent to material matters.[1] In a powerful expression of revolt, *The Tempests* lambasted the foibles of Easterners – their attachment to the past and to archaic traditions – advocated the emancipation of marriage and rejected all the chains bonding humanity. While he was on the side of the oppressed, Gibran rejected their submissiveness and weakness, and with Nietzschean momentum, encouraged them to aspire to power and greatness. Although a great believer in love, he rejected the notion that this emotion should control or enslave man.

In the aftermath several weeks later, Knopf published Gibran's second book in English, *The Forerunner*, with five of the author's own illustrations. Like *The Madman*, it was a collection of parables and stories replete with wisdom and mysticism. The forerunner that the author describes is a soul that has to outdo himself, to liberate himself from earthly desires, to attain the Absolute. 'Always have we been our own forerunners, and always shall we be. And all that we have gathered and shall gather shall be but seeds for fields yet unploughed. We are the fields and the ploughmen, the gatherers and the gathered.'

In 'The Last Evening', the forerunner, the one who claims to be the echo of a voice that has not yet been heard, announces the arrival of a yet bigger love. 'Night is over, and we children of night must die when dawn comes leaping upon the hills; and out of our ashes a mightier love shall rise. And it shall laugh in the sun, and it shall be deathless.'

---

1. Barbara Young confirms Gibran's lack of interest in his royalties and his great generosity in *This Man from Lebanon*, 1945, p. 32. Alfred Knopf's archives certify that Gibran used to pay careful attention to the artistic details of his books, but never discussed his royalties.

The book, less cynical and less vitriolic than the previous ones, paves the road for the author's masterpiece, *The Prophet*.

On 1 September 1920, a historical event took place in Lebanon. France obtained a mandate over Syria and Lebanon and proclaimed the existence of 'Greater Lebanon'. (Gibran considered France to be the most suitable European power to govern these regions as he blamed England for all the intrigues in the Middle East.) Greater Lebanon included the ancient territory of the Lebanese *mutassarefiat*; the coastal cities of Beirut, Tripoli, Sidon and Tyre; and the Bekaa Valley. It was at the Résidence des Pins that the famous General Gouraud, surrounded by the Maronite Patriarch and the Grand Mufti, proclaimed the creation of this state, whose flag would be three horizontal stripes (red, white, and red), with a cedar tree, the national emblem, in the centre of the middle, white stripe. Many Lebanese welcomed this historical decision, but Gibran regarded it with circumspection. In November 1919, he had already expressed his reserve at the hegemony of the great powers. 'International justice does not exist. I certainly do not want to lose faith in governments. But it seems sure that the fate of little nations will always find itself in the hands of more powerful, selfish, nations. The war has engendered more conscientiousness in men, but it has not created a deeper sense of rights and justice. It is still might that makes right.' On 8 November, he published his famous article, 'You have your Lebanon and I have mine' in *Al-Hilal*. In it, he confirms his love for Lebanon and its children and lashes out against politicians, who he feels have disfigured its image:

> You have your Lebanon with its dilemma. I have my Lebanon with its beauty. You have your Lebanon with all the conflicts rampant. I have my Lebanon with the dreams that live on. Your Lebanon is an international problem shot at by the shadows of the night. My Lebanon is made up of silent and

mysterious valleys whose sides absorb the chiming of the bells and the rustling of the brooks. Your Lebanon is a chess board for a religious leader and a military leader. My Lebanon is a temple that I visit in my spirit when my eyes weary of looking at this civilization on wheels. You have your Lebanon with its communities and political parties. My Lebanon is made up of boys who climb rocks and run with the streams. You have your Lebanon, I have mine.

Antagonised by this text, the Syrian authorities censored it from the magazines in which it appeared, but they forgot to rip out the table of contents, which included the title of the article and the name of the author. This act of censorship did not pass unnoticed and piqued the curiosity of the readers. 'I did not know that censorship in Syria was so poor,' Gibran wrote to the magazine owner. 'It makes me laugh and cry at the same time.'

Several months later, he did it again in an equally vociferous statement:

Pity the nation that wears a cloth it does not weave, eats a bread it does not harvest, and drinks a wine that flows not from its own winepress ...

Pity the nation divided into fragments, each fragment deeming itself a nation.[1]

Gibran, at this stage, was not idle. He was writing for the magazine *The Dial* and worked relentlessly on the manuscript of *The Prophet*, for which his publisher, Alfred Knopf, was clamouring. Gibran's health was deteriorating; his heart was acting up. 'It's all because my heart has lost its rhythm and meter. As you know, Mikhail, this heart has never beat to the rhythm of other hearts,' he wrote to Mischa. A doctor diagnosed him with a depression caused by overexertion and

1.   *Al-Hilal*, February 1923; *The Garden of the Prophet*, chapter 3.

malnutrition, a general disorder of his system, and a pulse that reached 115 heartbeats per minute. His only respite was contemplation of the sky. He bought himself a telescope to observe 'the infinite'. He was a little like Galileo, who, although debilitated with pain, never tired of scanning the skies.

Seeing him in this state, his friends took him out of 'The Hermitage', as they affectionately called his apartment, for a while and accompanied him to Cahoonzie, to a farm at the foot of the Catskill Mountains in eastern New York state. This little escapade in the company of Mischa, Arida and Haddad gave him much joy. For ten days, the four friends walked in nature, drank *arak*, sang, and improvised poems. They took photos which Gibran later good-naturedly demanded from Naimy. 'What happened to those pictures we took at Cahoonzie? I am hereby claiming one copy of each photo. If I do not obtain my rights, I will sue you in two courts: the court of friendship and the court of Ahmad Pacha el-Jazzar!'

But this outing was not enough to reinvigorate the weakened body of the artist. Upon returning to town, he had to take to his bed. He decided to stay in Boston, near his sister Mariana, the faithful Mariana, who had remained single all her life so she would always be available to take care of him.

It is during this period that Mary received a marriage proposal from a widower who had been married to a cousin of hers who had just died. The suitor's name was Florance Jacob Minis. He was sixty-nine years old and the president of an important railway company. Mary was no longer young. She knew she could no longer hope for anything from her protégé and dreaded spending the rest of her days in solitude. The prospect of moving to a luxurious mansion in Savannah, Georgia, in the company of an old but courteous man did not repel her. She eventually told Gibran that she had decided to accept the proposal. 'The relationship between you and me is the most wonderful thing

I have ever known in my life. It is eternal,' replied Gibran, and he added, 'I am happy because you are happy.' But Florance Jacob Minis was jealous and saw Gibran as a rival. From then on, the two friends were able to see each other less and less frequently.

Ironically, it was also during this period that Gertrude Barrie told him that she, too, had decided, at the age of forty-one, to get married. The lucky man was Hector Bazzinello, an Italian violinist passionate about aviation. Undoubtedly saddened to see his friend leave him, Gibran repeated what he had said to Mary, 'Your friends are happy to see you happy.' As if that were not enough, his sadness was compounded when he learned about the death of his friend, Posy. Josephine Peabody, one of his first great loves, died at the age of forty-eight from a long, drawn-out sickness. Finding himself alone, his friendship with the young photographer, Mariita Giacobbe, whom he met by chance in 1917, soothed his aching heart a little. She had sparkling eyes, a prominent nose, a firm chin and an irresistibly charming smile. She posed for Gibran, and he called her his 'sweet princess' and considered himself a sort of uncle to her. He wrote her tender letters in which he encouraged her to live out her dreams and celebrate life. 'I have forgotten the artists that I model for, except for Gibran,' she said towards the end of her life.[1]

Another consolation was his friendship with Witter Bynner, who was nicknamed 'Hal' by his friends, including Gibran. Gibran's letters to Bynner, whom he affectionately called 'Beloved Bynner' are a testimony to their complicity. Gibran talked to him about his health problems, admitting he had had a nervous depression, and about the situation in the East. Secluded in Santa Fe, Bynner dedicated to the Bsharri boy a play entitled *Cycle: A Play of War* in 1922.

---

1. Born in 1903, Mariita Lawson, née Giacobbe, later married and had a son. She visited Gibran's tomb in Lebanon in the 1970s.

Gibran's only goal was to finish *The Prophet* and return to his native country. That was not to be, however, because a major obstacle stood in his way. Despite the death of his father, creditors were still trying to track down the family. Sparing no one and nothing – as the local proverb said, 'Take from the bankrupt anything; even if it is only a handful of earth' – they were determined to find the heirs of Khalil Gibran and his sister Mariana, address unknown, and when they could not, they auctioned off all the family goods. This fact was confirmed by four warrants made in the executive court of the *caza* of Batroun, published in the *Official Newspaper*, and found later among the documents of the National Archives of Lebanon.[1] But Gibran never lost faith. 'May God spare us from civilisation and the civilised,' he confided in Mischa, 'We will return to the pure hills of Lebanon and its calm valleys. We will eat its herbs and grapes. We will sleep in its fields, wander with its flocks, and stay up listening to the sound of the shepherd's flutes and the murmur of its streams.' Nostalgia was his only outlet.

---

1. It is thanks to the cooperation of Hyam Mallat that we are able to access these public announcements in the *Official Newspaper* (no. 429 of 16 April 1912; no. 488 of 1 October 1912; no. 529 of 23 January 1913; and no. 601 of 12 August 1913).

THIRTEEN

The Prophet

*I*t took Gibran twenty years to write *The Prophet*. From his earliest childhood, the idea of the book had been brewing, but his mother had cautioned him to let the ideas ferment before launching himself into such an ambitious project. He changed the title four times and, until 1918, the book had not made real progress. In a letter to May Ziadeh on 9 November 1919, Gibran wrote, 'As for *The Prophet*, this is a book which I thought of writing a thousand years ago, but I did not get any of its chapters down on paper until the end of last year.' It is obvious that the artist had placed a great deal of importance on this incipient book. For him, it represented his rebirth, his first baptism, so to speak. From 1919 to 1923 Gibran dedicated most of his time to this work that he considered so essential. He met with Mary Haskell on several occasions, in Boston, New York, and Cambridge, to edit the text and make the corrections she suggested. Mary's judgment was sound; it reassured him. In 1923, feeling at last that the manuscript was adequately polished, he submitted it to his editor, Alfred Knopf, who had started to become impatient. The book finally appeared in September 1923.

The Prophet reads like a holy book. Its style, its structure and its tone are somewhat similar to those of the Bible, particularly the Gospels. Rich in imagery, allusions and parables, it is written in verse beginning with phrases like 'Verily' and 'I tell you'. The use of 'And' and 'For' to start many sentences lends the work a sense of solemnity. It uses Biblical figures, such as the unfaithful woman or the sinner, and rhetorical questions to make a philosophical point. 'Isn't regret justice administered by the same law that you pretend to follow?' These features are reminiscent of the Biblical style, just as the poetic prose of his friend, Amin Rihani, shares a similarity with the Koranic style. This phenomenon, in Gibranian writing, is not new: his writing between 1905 and 1908 abounds in biblical allusions and expressions culled from the *Psalms, Song of Songs, Ecclesiastes* and *The Book of Job*. In his own book, *Spirits Rebellious*, he includes several references from the New Testament. In the same vein, *The Forerunner* contains clear Biblical references, like the image of bread and wine, or expressions like 'on earth as it is in heaven' and 'Verily I say unto you'.

There are parallels between *The Prophet* and Nietzsche's *Thus Spake Zarathustra*, too. First of all, it is incontestable that Gibran had read and admired the work of the great German thinker before writing *The Prophet*. In a letter to Mary Haskell on 11 May 1911, Gibran wrote, 'I am delighted that you are reading *Zarathustra*. I need to read it with you in English.' On 30 August 1913, he wrote, 'Nietzsche took his words from my spirit. He picked the fruit from the tree I was heading towards.' Following Nietzsche's example, Gibran chose a wise man addressing the crowds as spokesperson to tackle different questions of interest to the author. In Nietzsche's book, Zarathustra, after ten years of solitude in the Alps, is prepared to share the fruit of his wisdom with people and decides to climb down the mountain. Gibran has Al-Mustafa wait twelve years for the return of the ship that is meant to take him back to his native island. He then comes down the hill just before his departure, to address the men and women of Ophalese. The themes tackled by both 'prophets' are similar: marriage, children, friendship, giving, freedom, crime, death ... and the same imagery is prevalent in both works, like the bow and arrow, the wanderer, the dancer or the stag.

But the similarity ends there. While the style of Nietzsche's writing, according to some critics, is burdened with heavy symbolism and emphatic eloquence, Gibran's *The Prophet* is lithe, limpid, disarmingly simple and impregnated with an Eastern spirit that never wanes. 'Nietzsche had an analytic mind,' observed Gibran himself, 'and the analytic mind always says too much.' In the domain of content, the differences by far outweigh the similarities. Whereas Nietzsche claims that God is dead ('All the gods are dead; what we want now is that the superhuman live') Gibran brings everything back to God. Whereas Nietzsche extols the transmutation of all values in order for an *Ubermensch* to take over decadent humanity, Gibran calls for aspiration to a 'Giant Self' by opening our hearts to love and invites us to a mystical flight towards the perfect world. There is not a single trace of nihilism in Gibran; *The Prophet* is a book that abounds in hope and optimism, something quite surprising coming from a man whose letters constantly allude to his failing health, his lack of well-being and his financial problems. In *Thoughts and Meditations* he writes, 'We, we are searching for the ghost of a hope.' Nietzsche was more of a philosopher (albeit his philosophy was described as lyrical) than Gibran, who never claimed to formulate his ideas in a single system. Finally, there is a lot of politics in Nietzsche's work. *Thus Spake Zarathustra* champions the cause of a social organisation, cruelly aristocratic and wildly anti-establishment, whereas Gibran's work has a completely different focus.

In reading *The Prophet*, one cannot help thinking about Herman Hesse's *Siddhartha*, published in 1922. Recreating India as a setting, Hesse condemns the world for its obsession with power and money, and, through writing soberly sprinkled with dialogue, sings the praises of a life of meditation. 'Bit by bit, Siddhartha develops an exact notion of wisdom. It is nothing but a predisposition of the soul, a capacity, a mysterious art that consists of identifying each moment of life with Oneness, to feel this Oneness everywhere, like the air that we breathe in our lungs.' It is as if Gibran himself could have written this. 'For me, there is only one important thing: to love the world, not to scorn it, not to hate anything and end up hating myself, to be able to unite in my love, in my admiration and in my respect, all the beings of the earth without excluding myself.' Al-Mustafa could have said these same words spoken by Siddhartha.

The Prophet has been criticised for being flat, simplistic, full of sentimentalism and riddled with the commonplace. That is not accurate, or else its continued popularity would be unexplainable or would have been disproved. The style of *The Prophet* is fluid; it flows. With poetry, Gibran delivers a spiritual message inviting the reader to the fulfilment of the self and a deeper thirst for life. The reader is literally captivated by the rhythm that enhances Gibran's verses:

> Say not, 'I have found the truth', but rather, 'I have found a truth.'
> Say not, 'I have found the path of my soul.'
> Say rather, 'I have met the soul walking upon my path.'
> For the soul walks upon all paths.
> The soul walks not upon a line, neither does it grow like a reed.
> The soul unfolds itself, like a lotus of countless petals.

In *The Prophet*, the meaning of the metaphors, allegories and symbols is mysterious without being cabalistic. The reader looks for the true substance and develops his own meaning. For Gibran, in spite of the commanding tone that Al-Mustafa uses, he does not profess intangible truths. One has 'to leave the reader the possibility of having his own word to say,' he wrote to Mary. 'I really prefer hidden truth to apparent truth,' he adds in a letter to May Ziadeh. In *The Prophet*, his character warns his disciples, 'If these be vague words, then seek not to clear them. Vague and nebulous is the beginning of all things, but not their end. And I fain would have you remember me as a beginning.'

In fact, to read Gibran well, one has to acquire what he calls 'a third eye' or rather 'the eye of the eye', the eye of the heart, the one that allows the reader to see through the darkness, which is 'vision, clairvoyance, particular understanding of things which are deeper than the depths, higher than the heights'.

But what does *The Prophet* tell us that we don't already know? Before his departure to 'the land of his remembrances', the prophet Al-Mustafa (an Arabic word meaning 'the chosen one, the well-loved by God') answers questions that are asked by humble citizens, the lovers, the mother and father, the priests, the lawyers, the businessmen ... and, surely, the female seer al-Mitra, probably inspired by the Persian divinity, Mithra, symbol of light, mediator among men and the supreme deity. By way of testament, he holds forth on lessons about life and makes wise recommendations which he expresses in terms such as:

> Love possesses not nor would it be possessed;
> For love is sufficient unto love.
> When you love, you should not say, 'God is in my heart,' but
>   rather, 'I am in the heart of God.'
> And think not you can direct the course of love, for love, if it
>   finds you worthy, directs your course.

About marriage, he holds forth with open-mindedness, in words that are used by couples every year in their wedding ceremonies.

Aye, you shall be together even in the silent memory of God.
But let there be spaces in your togetherness,
And let the winds of the heavens dance between you.
Love one another, but make not a bond of love:
Let it rather be a moving sea between the shores of your
souls ...
Fill each other's cup but drink not from one cup ...
And stand together yet not too near together:
For the pillars of the temple stand apart,
And the oak tree and the cypress grow not in each other's
shadow.

And on children, Al-Mustafa says:

Your children are not your children.
They are the sons and daughters of Life's longing for itself.
They come through you but not from you,
And though they are with you yet they belong not to you.
You may give them your love but not your thoughts,
For they have their own thoughts.
You may house their bodies but not their souls,
For their souls dwell in the house of tomorrow, which you
cannot visit, not even in your dreams.
You may strive to be like them, but seek not to make them
like you.
For life goes not backward nor tarries with yesterday.
You are the bows for which your children as living arrows are
sent forth.
The archer sees the mark upon the path of the infinite, and
He bends you with his might that His arrows may go swift
and far.
Let your bending in the Archer's hand to be for gladness;
For even as He loves the arrow that flies, so He loves also the
bow that is stable.

Readers are charmed by the boldness of his ideas and by the simplicity of his expression. It is no wonder that this work is known all over the world.

On work, Gibran goes off the beaten track. He has Al-Mustafa say:

> You have been told also that life is darkness, and in your
> weariness you echo what was said by the weary.
> And I say that life is indeed darkness save when there is urge,
> And all urge is blind save when there is knowledge,
> And all knowledge is vain save when there is work,
> And all work is empty save when there is love;
> And when you work with love you bind yourself to yourself,
> and to one another, and to God.

In the same vein that he affirms that 'life and death are one and the same, like the sea and the river are one,' Gibran claims that joy and sorrow are the same, and that the two notions are complementary and fuse together – an idea that is echoed in the parable of the two hunters in *The Wanderer*.

> Your joy is your sorrow unmasked.
> And the self-same well from which your laughter rises was
> oftentimes filled with your tears.
> And how else can it be?
> The deeper that sorrow carves into your being, the more joy
> you can contain.

And in the same manner in which he considers that 'evil is good tortured by its own hunger and its thirst,' he says about crime and punishment, 'the erect and the falling are but one man standing in twilight between the night of his pigmy-self and the day of his god-self.' As everything is in everything, it is all about keeping things in balance. (The image of the scale recurs more than once in his writing and is even the subject of a drawing entitled *Scales of the Absolute*.)

It is also about harmonising, conciliating and reconciling opposites to reach oneness. It was, after all, Gibran, using *The Prophet* as a mouthpiece, who advocated 'turning the discord and rivalry of the diverse elements in oneness and melody'.

The Prophet could have included an apologia for freedom, but he preferred to qualify his position and warn people against the chains of freedom, considering it as a means, and not as an end in itself:

> At the city gate and by your fireside I have seen you prostrate yourself and worship your own freedom,
> Even as slaves humble themselves before a tyrant and praise him though he slays them.
> Ay, in the grove of the temple and in the shadow of the citadel I have seen the freest among you wear their freedom as a yoke and a handcuff.
> And my heart bled within me; for you can only be free when even the desire of seeking freedom becomes a harness to you, and when you cease to speak of freedom as a goal and a fulfillment.

On pain, Gibran reminds us of Baudelaire's famous line, 'Be blessed, my God, for giving us suffering as a divine remedy for our impurities.'

> Much of your pain is self-chosen.
> It is the bitter potion by which the physician within you heals your sick self.
> Therefore trust the physician, and drink his remedy in silence and tranquility:
> For his hand, though heavy and hard, is guided by the tender hand of the Unseen, and the cup he brings, though it burn your lips, has been fashioned of the clay which the Potter has moistened with His own sacred tears.

About knowledge, Gibran shows himself to be open, describing 'the self' as 'the immeasurable, boundless sea.'

And on death, Al-Mustafa says these words with rare beauty:

> For what is it to die but to stand naked in the wind and to melt into the sun?
> And what is it to cease breathing, but to free the breath from its restless tides, that it may rise and expand and seek God unencumbered?
> Only when you drink from the river of silence shall you indeed sing.
> And when you have reached the mountaintop, then you shall begin to climb.
> And when the earth shall claim your limbs, then shall you truly dance.

Finally, at the moment of departure, Al-Mustafa addresses his disciples with a message full of hope and an invitation to believe in the self:

> You are not enclosed in your bodies nor confined to houses or fields. That which is you dwells above the mountain and roves with the wind. It is not a thing that crawls into the sun for warmth or digs holes into darkness for safety, but a thing free, a spirit that envelops the earth and moves in the ether.

❦

In 1931, Gibran wrote that *The Prophet* had been a part of his whole life and that he wanted to be absolutely certain that each word was the best possible one he could have used. His effort was not in vain: seventy-five years after his death, *The Prophet* is still read by millions of readers. What was his secret? This little book gives answers to people who are in search of a spirituality they can't find, or do not know how to find, in a modern society worn down by materialism, superficiality and anxiety, or in institutionalised religions. Gibran was able to condense wisdom of all religions in a work with a universal message. It belongs to no school, and dislikes 'isms'. For him, the only doctrine that was worth defending was the doctrine of life itself. One day he said to Barbara Young, 'I am a life-ist.' Bard of life – as 'life is hope itself' – the author of *The Prophet* chanted life till the very end.

FOURTEEN

The Winged Self

*G*ibran mentions God incessantly in all of his writings, particularly in *The Prophet*. He refers to him variously as The Powerful, The Guardian of the Night, The Heavenly Tree, The Archer, The Potter, and The Master Spirit of the Earth. Everything converges towards Him: prayer, love, passion, death, talent, work. Might one even consider agreeing with Barbara Young that Gibran was a 'Christian mystic'?[1] A Maronite Christian raised by a conservative and believing mother, educated by Father Semaan and then the priests at Al-Hikma College, Gibran was certainly well versed in Christianity and the Bible, his copy of which is still preserved in the museum at Bsharri. Interestingly enough, though, his knowledge of theology never developed into respect for the Church. Gibran was ulcerated by the coercive authoritarianism of some ecclesiastics and their wealth at a time of shortage. He was inspired by William Blake, who believed that priests 'tie up joy and desire in a bramble'. He was also influenced by Amin Rihani (author of the anticlerical novel, *The Book of Khalid*, published in New York, 1911) who relentlessly called for religious tolerance and the privatisation of the faith. Gibran directed his

---

1.   Barbara Young, *This Man from Lebanon*, 1945, p. 94.

venom against the clergy in most of his earlier writing, for example 'Youhanna the Madman' in *The Nymphs of the Valley* or 'Khalil the Heretic' in *Spirits Rebellious*. 'They sell prayer and those who refuse to buy are considered atheists and heathens and heaven is denied to them.' Gibran drew parallels between compassion and Christ's objectivity, and the grudges and pettiness of the clergy, and in *Broken Wings*, he did not hesitate to compare the prelates to octopuses!

What kind of God did Gibran believe in? His view of God was not mainstream. Gibran's mysticism is a convergence of several different influences: Christianity, Islam, Sufism, theosophy and Jungian psychology. It finds its echo in the works of Nietzsche, Blake, André Gide, Maeterlinck, Renan, Emerson and Whitman, whom he knew well, and Hesse, whom he had probably read. He was a native of Lebanon, which, contrary to appearances, represented religious syncretism, a message of coexistence and, to use a phrase coined by Salah Stétié, 'an ecumenical promise of peace'. He rejected fanaticism and religious segregation of any kind and culled his own convictions from a synthesis of different religious messages without their dogmatism. He asserted that religion is 'a natural belief in mankind' and could not reasonably confine himself to any one of the three great monotheistic religions. He writes,

> Your doctrine claims Mosaism, Brahmanism, Christianity, Islam. My doctrine says, 'There is but one single, abstract and absolute religion in multiple manifestations.'

And the beautiful passage:

> You are my brother and I love you. I love you when you prostrate yourself in your mosque, and kneel in your church, and pray in your synagogue. You and I are sons of one faith – the Spirit. And those that are set up as heads over its many

branches are as fingers on the hand of a divinity that points to
the Spirit's perfection.

In fact, as Jad Hatem explains in his analysis of *Iram, City of Lofty
Pillars*, 'The mystique of Gibran is meta-religious in that the characters
are trying to transcend the oversimplified perspectives of this or that
religion to embrace what they have in common.' It is not surprising,
therefore, that one of Gibran's drawings from 1918 is entitled *Crucified
on the Tower of Humanity and Religions* and depicts Christ, Buddha
and the great wise men of humanity.

According to Gibran, man does not know how to strip himself
down to his bare essence. He has to outdo himself, to forge ahead with
an ardent desire (the *shawq* of the Sufis) towards his divine self, and to
aspire to universal unity where everything reintegrates in a unique and
total hymn: the unity which is none other than God. Similarly, the
self, after having travelled the path leading to God, would merge with
Him. 'Man,' he writes in *Gods of the Earth*, 'is God in slow arising.' In
a letter to Mary Haskell dated 30 January 1916, he defines his thought
more precisely, 'God desires man and earth to become like Him, and
a part of Him. God is growing His desire, and man and earth, and all
there is upon earth rise towards God by the power of desire.'

Gibran's God is inherent to humanity as well as to nature. Likewise,
all Gibran's work basks in an atmosphere of pantheism. His paintings,
like his writing, make constant reference to Mother Nature: *Mother
Discovering Nature, The Woman in Harmony with Nature, Man
and the Symphony of Nature, The Spirit of the Mother Manifesting
Itself in Nature*. Many canvases reflecting the ideas of the artist use the
centaur as the symbol of Mother Nature: *Feminine and Motherly
Nature, Nature Leaning over Man, His Son*; and as the image of the

double nature of man, his beastliness and his divinity. 'Nature is but the form of God, His body,' he confides in Mary, 'and God is what I sing and what I want to understand.' For him, beauty has metaphysical dimensions: it is a transcendent entity which brings to Man the sense of reality; it is the tangible manifestation of the invisible.[1] 'Are you lost in the valley of beliefs in conflict? Make beauty your religion, for it is the visible, perfect manifestation of God.'

For Gibran, God is an undeniable reality with nature being the tangible expression of God behind all the apparent manifestations. Beings do not exist except through Him. All communication with Him passes through nature, which becomes the means of a mystical experience, where across trees, rivers and light, the self breaks the frontiers that separate him from the All to fuse with the totality of existence in a feeling of unification.[2]

> All things in this creation exist within you, and all things in you exist in creation; there is no border between you and the closest things, and there is no distance between you and the farthest things, and all things, from the lowest to the loftiest, from the smallest to the greatest, are within you as equal things. In one atom are found all the elements of the earth; in one motion of the mind are found the motions of all the laws of existence; in one drop of water are found the secrets of all the endless oceans; in one aspect of you are found all the aspects of existence.

This vision of the world is appealing. It matches perfectly Alain's[3] definition of pantheism in *The Arts and the Gods*. 'It is the religion of nature that takes cult objects in all its forces ... that are considered

---

1. Najib Zakka, 'The Metaphysics of Gibran', in *Contemporary Lebanese Literature*, USEK, 2000, pp. 428–30.
2. Souad Kharrat, *Gibran the Prophet, Nietzsche the Visionary*, Triptyque, 1993, p. 90.
3. Emile Chartier, alias Alain, is a French philosopher (1868-1951.)

as manifestations of a single God, and who is the world. Pantheism means that all is god and that it is the all which is God.' This brings to mind the Sufi poet, Rumi:

> Why do you not want that the part is reunited with the whole, the beam of light with the light? In my heart I hold the universe, around me the world holds me.[1]

A passage from *The Madman* confirms the notion that God is found in all manifestations of life.

> In the ancient days, when the first quiver of speech came to my lips, I ascended the holy mountain and spoke unto God, saying, 'Master, I am thy slave ...' but God made no answer, and like a mighty tempest passed away. And after a thousand years I ascended the holy mountain again and spoke unto God, saying, 'Creator, I am thy creation. Out of clay hast thou fashioned me and to thee I owe mine all.' And God made no answer, but like a thousand swift wings passed away. And after a thousand years I climbed the holy mountain and spoke unto God again, saying, 'Father, I am thy son. In pity and love thou has given me birth, and through love and worship I shall inherit thy kingdom.' And God made no answer, and like the mist that veils the distant hills he passed away. And after a thousand years I climbed the sacred mountain and again spoke unto God, saying, 'My God, my aim and my fulfillment; I am thy yesterday and thou art my tomorrow. I am thy root in the earth and thou art my flower in the sky, and together we grow before the face of the sun.' Then God leaned over me, and in my ears whispered words of sweetness, and even as the sea that enfoldeth a brook that runneth down to her, he enfolded me. And when I descended to the valleys and the plains God was there also.

---

1. Jean Chevalier, *Le Soufisme*, PUF, p. 64.

In between naturalistic pantheism and divine humanism, the text aptly summarises the thoughts of its author. Here, God and Man unite; God appears as the fulfilment of Man, his domain, his 'winged self'. Along the same lines, in *The Prophet* Gibran has Al-Mustafa say,

> And if you would know God be not therefore a solver of riddles.
> Rather look about you and you shall see Him playing with your children.
> And look into space; you shall see Him walking in the cloud, outstretching His arms in the lightning and descending in rain.
> You shall see Him smiling in flowers, then rising and waving His hands in trees.

And in *The Garden of the Prophet*, he has his main character saying,

> I would like to know that we are the breath and the fragrance of God. We are God in the leaf, in the flower, and often also in the fruit.

This mélange of ideas led Gibran to metempsychosis, or reincarnation. Although he never actually used this term, he believed in the 'continuity of life'. Inspired by the Hindu theory of reincarnation of the soul in purifying steps until the final fusion in the absolute, Gibran adopted, like the key to survival of the soul, the idea of eternal return.[1]

> Forget not that I shall come back to you.
> A little while, and my longing shall gather dust and foam for another body.

---

1. In J. Head and S.L. Cranston's work, *The Book of Reincarnation* (1991), Gibran is cited among a number of authors who envisaged or admitted the belief or the hope for reincarnation..

A little while, a moment of rest upon the wind, and another
woman shall bear me.

In a letter to Mary Haskell dated 8 June 1924, he wrote, 'In myself
I have experiences that indicate previous lives to me. I am perfectly
certain I have known you for thousands of years.' Where did this
idea come from? Undoubtedly, from the pain of seeing his first love,
Sultana Tabet, and then his sister, his half-brother, his mother, and
his father die in succession, and the hope that they would live again.
Reincarnation, a belief held by two religious communities in Lebanon
and Syria, the Druzes and the Alaouites, as well as by thousands
of Mormons in the USA, created an imaginary means to avoid the
anguish of death and offered the promise of another life, a survival,
an 'eternal return'. In addition, the influence of Nietzsche, and that
of his friends Mikhail Naimy and Charlotte Teller, the theosophist,
both reinforced this idea. Furthermore, there was an advantage: this
egalitarian doctrine promised social repercussions. In the next life,
the riches of today would belong to the downtrodden tomorrow, and
vice versa. Omnipresent in Gibran's work, the theme is first broached
in the poetry of *Thoughts and Meditations*.

> O Soul, what is life if it is not a night that fades until it
> becomes dawn, and dawn continues. O Soul, if sometimes
> the madman says, 'The soul perishes like the body, and what
> happens between life and death does not come back,' then he
> would answer, 'The flowers die, but the seeds remain.' And
> that is where the essence of eternity lies.

And where is Jesus in all of this? For Gibran, Jesus of Nazareth was
not the Jesus of the Christians.

> Once every hundred years, Jesus of Nazareth meets Jesus of
> the Christian among the hills of Lebanon,

> And they talk long, and each time Jesus of Nazareth goes away
> saying to Jesus of the Christian, 'My friend, I fear we shall
> never, never agree.'

In *The Prophet*, Al-Mustafa seems to shadow the Messiah. The face figuring on the frontispiece of the original edition of the text, and for which Gibran had a particular fondness, bears a striking resemblance to depictions of Jesus Christ. In *The Garden of the Prophet*, which is a sequel, Al-Mustafa isolates himself for forty days as Jesus had done in the desert after his baptism; his nine disciples call to mind the twelve apostles of Christ; and the final retreat of seven days reminds us of the night on the Mount of the Olives. In *Jesus, the Son of Man*, Gibran deals with the Christ that his protector Fred Holland Day represented in his photographs and that he himself saw often in his dreams. Probably inspired by the Ernest Renan's *Vie de Jésus* (*Life of Jesus*), where the Messiah appears like 'a man who by his example took the biggest step towards the divine,' he emphasised the human nature of Jesus:

> He was not a god, He was a man like unto ourselves. But in
> Him the myrrh of the earth rose to meet the frankincense
> of the sky; and in His words, our lisping embraced the
> whispering of the unseen; and in His voice, we heard a song
> unfathomable. Aye, Jesus was a man and not a god; and
> therein lies our wonder and our surprise.

Elsewhere in the text, he writes,

> Now you would know why some of us call Him the Son of
> Man. He Himself desired to be called by that name, for He
> knew the hunger and the thirst of man, and He beheld man
> seeking after His greater self. The Son of Man was Christ
> the Gracious, who would be with us all. He was Jesus the
> Nazarene who would lead His brothers to the Anointed One,
> even to the Word which was in the beginning with God. In

my heart dwells Jesus of Galilee, the Man above men, the Poet who makes poets of us all, the Spirit who knocks at our door that we may wake and rise and walk out to meet truth naked and unencumbered.

Gibran is fascinated by the principles of love and freedom that Jesus advocated and the new set of values that emerged from them.

Jesus was not a bird with broken wings; He was a raging tempest who broke all crooked wings. Jesus was not sent here to teach people how to build magnificent churches and temples amidst the cold, wretched huts and dismal hovels ... He came to make the human heart a temple, and the soul an altar, and the mind a priest.

Gibran admits that Jesus is immortal. But it is not because he is God that he is immortal. It is because he knew how to follow the path that leads to the divine. Mankind has achieved, with and through Jesus, the perfect divine manifestation. In this, Gibran heralded Nikos Kazantzakis, who in *The Last Temptation of Christ* shows us a human Christ who walks endlessly towards the heights, to attain salvation for humanity and who, through long, harsh experience, achieves unity with God. Gibran strays from the dogmas of the Catholic Church as he calls into question the consubstantiation of the Father and the Son and de-emphasises the redemption and the Eucharist. But for all that, his thesis is not so radical: well versed in the Bible, Gibran has a high opinion of Jesus and wrote texts about Him with such beauty that it is difficult to think of him as a heretic or a vulgar 'guru' of the New Age.[1] Barbara Young was not mistaken when she said that Gibran was a 'Christian mystic', after a fashion.

---

1. Robin Waterfield (*Prophet: The Life and Times of Kahlil Gibran*, 1998, p. 289) considers Gibran to be an 'unknown inspirer of the New Age'..

FIFTEEN

Let Me Sleep

On the whole, the press received *The Prophet* enthusiastically. Gibran's earlier book, *Thoughts and Meditations*, published in Cairo in 1923, was an anthology of some of his Arabic articles, maxims, literary portraits, parables and sociopolitical editorials, among which was the famous 'You have your Lebanon ...' Gibran was relieved at the success of *The Prophet* because *Thoughts and Meditations* had been vociferously criticised by the Jesuit priest Louis Cheikho, who went as far as to accuse him of being a freemason.[1] Could he possibly have been one? His signature, some of the symbols he used and the company he kept might lead one to think so. His signature consisted of three dots inside the centre of three intersecting circles, or a circle with the letter K inside it, and in Freemasonry, the three dots symbolise the Delta. Then there is the 'divine eye', which is found in his painting entitled *The Divine World*, symbolising the Grand Architect of the Universe. And the circles he moved in – Fred Holland Day and the Camera

---

1.   A recent book by G. Figuié, *Le Point sur la Franc-maçonnerie au Liban*, Anthologie, Beirut, 1998, states that Gibran was initiated in the Parisian Lodge, that he belonged to the American Freemasons, and that he was a member of the New York Lodge (p. 220). See also Khalil Kfoury's book in Arabic, *Gibran and Naimy, Freemasons*, Beirut, 2002.

Club which included a number of freemasons and theosophists, the Golden Circle, which he formed along Masonic lines, and his friend Amin Rihani, who was himself a freemason – may suggest some kind of allegiance. Indications, perhaps, but not proof. Gibran was too free-spirited to bind himself to any set doctrine. Undoubtedly, Cheikho's accusation had been intended to discredit Gibran for the sacrilegious ideas he propounded. However, a one-act play by Gibran entitled 'Iram, the City of Lofty Pillars' from *Best Things and Masterpieces*, is greatly spiritual. It is about a young writer by the name of Nageeb Rahmeh, who is searching for Amina the Alawite, the 'djinn of the valley', to question her about the mythical site of Iram that she had visited. Amina teaches Nageeb that he carries within him all of creation and that nothing ever perishes, and she insists that faith and imagination are essential to complement rational thought.

> Everything which is fixed in space and time is a spiritual state. Everything visible and everything intelligible are spiritual states. If you close your eyes and you look in the deepest recesses of your soul, you will see the world in its whole and in its details. Everything in existence is found in your essence, and everything in your essence is found in existence. In a single drop of water is found all the secrets of the seas, and in a single atom, all the elements on earth ... When you know a thing, you believe it, and the true believer sees with his spiritual discernment that which the surface investigator cannot see with the eyes of his head, and he understands through his inner thought that which the outside examiner cannot understand with his demanding, acquired process of thought. The believer acquaints himself with the sacred realities through deep senses different from those used by others.

The *Chicago Evening Post* critics praised *The Prophet* to the skies. 'The rhythm of Gibran's words are retained in our ears like the majestic book "Ecclesiastes". Kahlil Gibran is not afraid to be an idealist in an era abounding with cynicism. The twenty-eight chapters of this little bible are recommended reading to those who are more than ever ready to see the truth.' In the London *Times*, a journalist considered the work 'a synthesis of everything good in Christian thought and Buddhist thought'. Word of mouth was the best publicity: everybody was crazy about the book.[1] Gibran was invited everywhere. He was even invited to the Roosevelts' at Herkimer, where he met Franklin D., the future president of the USA. He also met the eminent British author, G. K. Chesterton, John Galsworthy (winner of the 1932 Nobel Prize in Literature) and the Mexican painter Jose Clemente Orozco. Soon afterwards, he was asked to serve as a member on the board of the prestigious magazine *New Orient Society*, which included Gandhi and Bertrand Russell, and whose aim was to bring the West and the East closer together 'in a spirit of spiritual and intellectual camaraderie'.

Gibran was finally famous, but his financial worries still hounded him. He had invested his money in a real estate project which ended up losing money, and he had, yet again, to ask Mary Haskell to help him settle his debts. In a letter sent to a friend from Boston[2] he expressed his irritation with this business. 'You should have seen me, Helena, in these stifling days, traipsing from lawyer's office to business center to litigation court and speaking a language I have never spoken before in my life ... If you had seen me like that, you would have sympathized with and had much affection for me.'

At forty-two, Gibran felt alone. Nostalgia gnawed at him. 'The day will come when I will be leaving for the Orient. My longing for my country almost melts my heart. Had it not been for this cage

---

1. In a letter dated January 29, 1926, Knopf wrote to Gibran: '*The Prophet* is going on beautifully.'
2. An undated letter to Helena Ghostine.

which I have woven with my own hands, I would have caught the first boat sailing towards the Orient. But what man is capable of leaving an edifice on whose construction he has spent all his life, even though that edifice is his own prison? It is difficult to get rid of it in one day.'

In a letter to Félix Farès,[1] he wrote, 'I must go back to Lebanon, and I must withdraw myself from this civilization which runs on wheels. However, I deem it is wise not to leave this country before I break the strings and chains that tie me down. I wish to go back to Lebanon and remain there forever.'

It was during this delicate period that two new women came into his life. The first was Henrietta Boughton, alias Barbara Young, a literary critic for *The New York Times* and author of several works published under various pseudonyms. She was four years his senior (to no one's surprise) and homely. The morning after the publication of *The Prophet*, Barbara Young was attending the reading of passages from this book by the actor Butler Davenport, in the Anglican church of Saint Mark's Church in-the-Bowery. Blown away by this work, she wrote to Gibran and asked to meet him. He invited her to his house, and when they met, there was immediate chemistry between them. For seven years, she remained his devoted secretary, writing and then typing what he dictated, arranging his papers and his belongings. After Mary, Barbara became his next guardian angel; but without the love.

The second woman to enter his life at this time was Helena Ghostine. Of Lebanese origin (she had emigrated from Bzébdine in 1917), she had perfect command of Arabic, English, and French, which she had learned at the Sorbonne. While teaching,[2] she wrote for

---

1. An intellectual and journalist, Félix Farès (1882–1939) was the translator into Arabic of *Rolla* and *The Confession of a Child of the Century* of Musset, and *Thus Spake Zarathustra* by Nietzsche.
2. One of the letters Gibran sent her on 12 January 1926 was addressed to Benjamin School, 145 Riverside Drive, New York City.

the New York newspaper *al-Houda*, founded by her maternal uncle, Naoum Mokarzel. Close to the US administration, she accomplished a vaguely defined mission during World War II which earned her a medal. Gibran had met her for the first time in the offices of *al-Houda*, where he used to go during the World War I.[1] Few letters, not well known, remain of those he sent her, and reveal the nature of their relationship. The artist admired her, affectionately called her 'My pretty girl', and often wanted her around.

> I loved your two photos, especially the little one ... Ah, if only I could become the friend of the woman in this superb photograph in flesh and blood! No problem. I will find this friend or her shadow in the world of spirits in between the folds of eternity ... I will be at home in New York on Wednesday September 5 at 8:00 p.m. And as I have important things to tell you, it would be a good idea for you to visit me that evening.

On a Wednesday evening three years later, he wrote to her from Boston, 'I have just come back from New York; I am still skinny, and am at the end of my tether. But I would like to see you. I hope you will call or write me. I know in my heart that you would not refuse to visit a man hurt, bruised, and in low spirits ... I want to thank you face to face and to tell you how grateful I am for all the affection and friendship you have shown me over the last three years.

Weakened by his illness and infuriated by the 'pilgrims' (to quote Barbara Young) who disrupted his serenity, Gibran found peace in Helena, his countrywoman. He knew he could count on her. In a letter written on 6 January 1925, he thanks her for the birthday present she had sent him. 'I thank you because you always remember my

---

1. The 12 April 2001 edition of *al-Hayat* quotes Ibrahim Nasser Soueidan about Helena.

birthday. Every year, on the same day, I feel in my heart a surrendering to the great power that wanted me to exist and who placed me in the face of the sun, and then that endowed me with faithful and devoted friends who allow me to forget my anguish and the melancholy in my soul ...' And, in another letter dated 12 January 1926, he asks her to help him organise a ceremony to pay tribute to Sleiman Bustani,[1] the scholar who had just passed away in New York. He describes him as a 'beautiful and great, pure soul'. When she seemed tired, he addressed her in a rather fatherly tone,

> You, Oh Helena, you complain although you have no cause for complaint. You whimper over the darkness even when you are sitting in the light of the sun, and you resent time although time is your ally.

Among the poems he sent her, there is one, dated 20 May 1923, which is revealing of his state of mind. 'They dug the nails deep into the palm of my hand ... and in my heart. There are chants that I can put to music only if their melodies mix with my blood.'

At the beginning of 1926, Alfred A. Knopf published Gibran's new book in English, *Sand and Foam*, an anthology of 322 aphorisms written on bits of paper, collected by Barbara Young. It included seven reproductions of his drawings and little illustrations between each maxim. A bit like Blake's *The Marriage of Heaven and Hell* or Maeterlinck's *Treasure of the Humble*, the work offers reflections on a variety of topics – love, friendship, desire, death, freedom, among others. It reveals, at times, a dualistic view of the world. For example, 'How can I lose faith in the justice of life, when the dreams of those who sleep upon feathers are not more beautiful than the dreams of

---

1. Sleiman Bustani (1856–1925) is the Arabic translator of Homer's *The Illiad*.

those who sleep upon the earth?' Or 'Birth and death are the two noblest expressions of bravery.' Profoundly simple and colourful, the aphorisms in this anthology make a strong impression on the reader.

Meanwhile, Gibran was working nonstop. When he wasn't writing or painting, he was sculpting little wooden objects. He wrote for the magazine *The Syrian World* (edited by Salloum Moukarzel), which included aphorisms and parables in English. It was in this magazine that he published his famous 'To the Americans of Syrian origin', an essay calling for his countrymen to feel pride in the duality of Eastern and Western belonging and the integration of new ideas without denying or rejecting their roots. Some time later, in a sudden burst of inspiration, he decided to abandon the project of writing a sequel to *The Prophet* and instead started a new book, *Jesus, the Son of Man*, which he dictated to Barbara Young. For eighteen months, he worked on this book which describes the hero, Christ, through the eyes of seventy characters from the Bible and from mythology.[1] Some of them love Jesus while others are indifferent, curious about, or hostile to him. The image composed by their testimony is of a fascinating person, superior, worthy of adoration, all the while remaining close to men, his brothers. On Mary's birthday (11 December) that year, 1927, he sent her the manuscript he had just finished. So as not to upset her husband, she read it clandestinely when he was asleep.

On 12 October the following year (1928), the work was published with fourteen illustrations by the author. The American press praised the book. 'Gibran's English is marked by a beauty and a clarity that can inspire other writers whose native language is English,' wrote the *Springfield Union*. A columnist from the *Manchester Guardian*

---

1. There is a similarity with Robert Browning's *The Ring and the Book*, a series of dramatic monologues in which various characters comment on the situation in which they find themselves.

guaranteed the reader would 'experience great joy when he discovers the book's original, particular, and beautiful sensuousness ...'

It is during this period that his old classmate, Ayub Tabet, Sultana's brother, returned to Lebanon and was appointed Lebanese Minster of Interior and of Health before becoming the President of the Republic. Gibran claimed that Tabet had offered him a ministerial post, but there is no evidence to corroborate that claim.[1]

Finding no alleviation for his aches and pains, Gibran took refuge in alcohol. In spite of the Prohibition, he consumed great quantities of *arak* and begged his sister to procure this liquor from a close friend, Assaf George, in the illegal distilleries of Chinatown in Boston. 'My thirst for wine surpasses that of Noah's, Abu Nuwas's and Debussy's, as well as Marlowe's.' But this remedy was also his poison. Drinking had killed his friend, Albert Ryder, and his own father. No matter! The gift of thirst had no price tag.

> Therefore drink your cup alone and in silence. The autumn days have given other lips cups and filled them with wine bitter and sweet, even as they have filled your cup. Drink your cup alone though it taste of your own blood and tears, and praise life for the gift of thirst. For without thirst your heart is but the shore of a barren sea, songless and without a tide. Drink your cup alone, and drink it with cheers. Raise it high above your head and drink deep to those who drink alone.

Gibran was aging prematurely. One photograph taken around that time, as well as a film of a few seconds of him smoking a cigarette at his table, shows the gravity of his condition. His hair had turned grey, he had circles under his eyes, his complexion was pallid and his face

---

1.   Walid Aouad, *The Lebanese Presidents (1926–1943)*, Dar al-Afkar, Beirut 2002, p. 288.

was puffy. But he held on. In a letter to May Ziadeh, he romanticised even his pain and suffering:

> I have pleasure in being ill. This pleasure differs with its effect from any other pleasure. I have found a sort of tranquility that makes me love illness. Through sickness I have found an even greater and more important pleasure. I have found that I am closer to abstract things in my sickness than in health. When I lay my head and close my eyes and lose myself to the world, I find myself flying like a bird over serene valleys and forests, wrapped in a gentle veil. I see myself close to those whom my heart has loved, calling and talking to them, but without anger and with the same feelings they feel and the same thoughts they think. They lay their hands now and then upon my forehead to bless me.

On 5 January 1929, his Pen League friends organised a dinner in his honour at the McAlpin Hotel in New York. They wanted to celebrate his twenty-five years of service to Arabic literature. A few days later, he underwent medical examinations that revealed an alarming hypertrophy of the liver. Radium radiation had no effect. Claiming he preferred to let nature take its due course, he refused to undergo surgery. 'It is a plight, Mischa, to be always between illness and health,' he wrote to Naimy in March 1929. 'The doctors warned me against working. Yet there is nothing I can do but work ... What would you think of a book composed of four stories on the lives of Michelangelo, Shakespeare, Spinoza, and Beethoven? What would you say if I showed their achievements to be the unavoidable result of pain, ambition, "expatriation," and hope moving in the human heart?'

Gibran knew that his days were numbered. He foreshadowed his own death in a letter to Mary in which he wrote that when he thought about that great departure most people call death, he could only think about it with a strange pleasure and great nostalgia. He put his affairs in order and on 13 March 1930 made out a new will. He left all his liquid assets and his forty shares in the real estate company that owned his studio on 51 West 10th Street to his sister, Mariana. To his native village, Bsharri, he left the revenue from all his books, and to Mary Haskell he left all his paintings, books, and artistic objects remaining in his studio, suggesting that she might, if she were to find it suitable, send them, wholly or in part, to Bsharri when she saw fit. In July, he rented a house on the seaside and spent two months there with his sister. He worked on a new book, *The Dervish*, which later became *The Wanderer*. Upon his return, he wrote to May Ziadeh that he knew his health had deteriorated since the beginning of the summer.

On 14 March, Alfred A. Knopf published *The Earth Gods*, his last book to be published during his lifetime. It is a Socratic dialogue among three gods representing the three great tendencies of the human heart. The first is tired of living like a god and aspires to the void. The second likes his condition and takes advantage of the power he wields over men who are 'the bread of the gods'. The third, rejecting the indifference of one and the arrogance of the other, rejoices in seeing a couple singing and dancing at the foot of the mountain, convinced that the secret of existence lies in beauty and love. He proclaims:

> They who are conquered by love,
> And upon whose bodies love's chariot ran
> From sea to mountain
> And again from mountain to the sea,
> Stand even now in a shy half-embrace.
> Petal unto petal they breathe the sacred perfume,
>   Soul to soul they find the soul of life,
> And upon their eyelids lies a prayer.

In this little book of about forty pages that carries Blake's stamp and the *Hyperion* of Keats, one finds the idea that the man of flesh can surpass himself and evolve towards god-man to unite with Him. The gods of the earth are those beings who left the sand for the mist, those who were able to transcend the narrow limits of their self to aspire to the absolute and melt into it. 'And the glory of man begins when his aimless breath is sucked by gods' hallowed lips.'

He sent Mary a copy, accompanied by the manuscript of *The Wanderer*. 'I wonder if you should care to see the manuscript with your seeing eyes and lay your knowing hands upon it before it is submitted. May God love you.' These were the last words ever addressed to the one who never stopped watching over him.

On 3 April, Gibran completed three drawings intended as illustrations for *The Wanderer* and three days later was visited by his friend, Abdul Massih Haddad. Haddad was appalled by Gibran's physical condition. 'For the first time, I heard death in his voice and saw it on his face. We talked of various things, but he kept referring to the Pen League and our fellow members. He named them one by one and bared his soul to bid them farewell. When he asked me about my family, he mentioned my children, one by one, and gave me money to buy my wife a bouquet of flowers in their name.' The countdown had started.

On Thursday, 9 April, the concierge in Gibran's studio, Anna Johansen, brought him his breakfast, as was her wont, and found him dying. She alerted the neighbour on the same landing, Leonobel Jacobs, who immediately called a doctor, but Gibran refused to be taken to hospital. The next day, at 10.30 AM, he lost consciousness. In a panic, Barbara Young drove him to Saint Vincent Hospital. His sister, his cousins, Mischa, the Maronite priest, Francis Wakim, and a few other friends rushed to see him. But it was too late: the cirrhosis of his liver and the tuberculosis in one lung had thrown Gibran into a deep coma.

On Friday, 10 April 1931, at 10.55 PM the author of *The Prophet* took his last breath. He was only forty-eight years old.

> O Mist, my sister, my sister Mist,
> I am one with you now.
> No longer am I a self.
> The winds have fallen,
> And the chains have broken;
> I rise to you, a mist,
> And together we shall float upon the sea until life's second day.
> When dawn shall lay you, dewdrops in a garden,
> And me a babe upon the breast of a woman.

On 12 April, Mary Haskell received a telegram from Mariana:

> KAHLIL PASSED AWAY FRIDAY NIGHT. WE TAKE HIM TO BOSTON ON MONDAY WRITE 28, FOREST HILLS, ST JAMAICA PLANS MASS.

She remained speechless, broken by the premature death of this being whom she had cherished so dearly. Like Mariana, Barbara, May, Mischa, and so many others, she cried for the loss of her friend and protégé. In a prose poem entitled, 'The Beauty of Death' he had written,

> Let me sleep, for my soul is intoxicated with love and
> Let me rest, for my spirit has had its bounty of days and nights ...
> Lament me not, but sing songs of youth and joy ...
> Draw upon my face with your finger the symbol of Love and Joy ...
> Talk not of my departure with sighs in your hearts;
> Close your eyes and you will see me with you forevermore.

SIXTEEN

After Death

'A prophet is dead' was one of the headlines in the *New York Sun* the following day. Gibran's body was taken to the Universal Funeral Parlor on Lexington Avenue, where it remained for two days before being transferred to Boston on Monday, 13 April, escorted by members of the *Rabita* and shortly afterwards by Mary. (Gibran had never made his relationship with Mary public and therefore had never deemed it wise to introduce her to his friends; consequently, she did not know any of them.) The next day, a funeral service was held at Our Lady of the Cedars by one of the very few priests of whom the deceased ever approved, Mgr Istiphan Douaihy, his neighbour and advisor. After the ceremony, the coffin was placed in the Monte Benedict Cemetery in a Bostonian suburb, where the remains of his mother, sister and half-brother had been laid to rest. As a farewell to the departed, several ceremonies were organised in New York, Buenos Aires and São Paolo, cities with large Lebanese communities. Shortly afterwards, upon the request of Mary Haskell, who had not forgotten her promise to him in August 1913, Mariana gave her consent for the body to be sent to Bsharri.

On 23 July 1931, a large number of friends and relatives saw Gibran's coffin, enveloped in both the Lebanese and American flags, leave the New World on a ship called *Sinaia*. When the coffin arrived in Beirut on Thursday, 20 August 1931, its reception by the local community was unprecedented. An official delegation, which included Commandant de Maurapas, a delegate of the French authorities, and a delegate from the French Marines, were waiting at the dock. The remains were received by Archbishop Ignatius Mobarak and displayed for a whole day in the Saint George Cathedral. After a ceremony at the Grand Theatre in homage to the deceased, in the presence of the head of state, Charles Debbas, the coffin was covered with olive branches and transported from village to village and escorted all the way up to Bsharri by a considerable crowd. According to a journalist there, the arrival of the crowd at the town looked more like a triumphant entrance than a funeral. The church bells and general atmosphere of pride reinforced this impression.[1]

On 10 January 1932, the cedarwood coffin was finally laid to rest in a grotto carved into the rocks in the interior of the Monastery of Mar Sarkis, which Mariana had bought at the request of her late brother and which today houses the Gibran Museum. Right beside his final resting place, his room with his remarkably small bed was reconstructed, and on the wall hung a small tapestry of Christ, the painter's easels, a few decorative items brought back from 'The Hermitage', and an inscription engraved on a wooden plaque: 'One word that I want written on my tomb: I am alive like you, and now I am by your side. Close your eyes, look around you, and you will see me.'

To the very end, Gibran denounced death as a means of cheating destiny and avenging those who had died before him.

---

1.   The ceremony was chronicled in detail by Habib Massoud, *Gibran Living and Dead*, ed. Rihani, 2nd ed., 1966, p. 527.

Meanwhile, in the US, the power struggles began. Barbara Young made an inventory of his work and considered destroying the letters he had received from Mary Haskell (about whom she had known nothing!) under the pretext that they tarnished the writer's reputation. Mary managed to salvage the letters concerning her *in extremis*, but she was powerless in the face of Barbara's interference with her protégé's work. She lived far from New York and had to look after her ailing husband. She passed away on 9 October 1964, at the age of ninety-one. She had spent the last five years of her life in a hospital and had given away all her assets, leaving her diary and her correspondence with Gibran for posterity, without which an entire chunk of his life would have remained undiscovered.

Barbara executed Gibran's will as she saw fit. *The Wanderer* and *The Garden of the Prophet* underwent major modifications under her pen. She took a sudden dislike to Mischa, forbade his Lebanese friends, namely the members of the *Rabita*, to consult the artist's archives, and asked for exorbitant sums for the paintings of the deceased while appropriating a number of them for herself. After going on a pilgrimage to Bsharri in 1939 'to retrace the prophet's footsteps', she wrote a laudatory biographical novel about him entitled *This Man from Lebanon*.[1]

As for Mariana, she contested her brother's will but ended up losing the lawsuit. In 1968, debilitated by illness, she resigned herself to living in a rest home. That is where she died on 28 March 1972, at the age of eighty-eight.

As if to confirm that he had never left, every now and again a previously unknown text by Gibran would surface. Published posthumously in 1932, *The Wanderer* is an anthology of parables that

---

1. In an unpublished letter to Knopf, dated July 22 1945, Barbara Young rejected the idea of translating *Broken Wings* into English deeming the book to be too rebellious.

relates the roaming of the thinker through his regrets and is a quasi-sequel to *The Madman* and *The Forerunner*. With a tone at times ironic or disenchanted, the author touches on all the topics he held dear to his heart: love, truth, nature and God. In one of the parables, entitled 'The Hermit Prophet', Gibran tells the story of a prophet who preaches giving and sharing. One day, three men come into his hermitage (and the allusion is intentional) asking him to share his riches. Now the prophet had no riches, so the men disparaged him, saying, 'Oh you cheat, you imposter! You teach and preach what you yourself do not practise!' Haunted by the desire to live up to the image that his work reflected or that others had of him, Gibran needed to exorcise his dread of failure. Mikhail Naimy reported that Gibran had once confessed to him 'I am a false alarm', undoubtedly blurted out during a moment of self-doubt. The parable of the hermit prophet explicitly exposes the discrepancy between image and reality. Whatever a prophet does, he is always accused and suspected of imposture. Gibran, in point of fact, never pretended to be a paragon of virtue. All his work shows he is conscious of his own weaknesses. In the text 'Love', he talks about the 'weak self', and he does not place himself above others. Like *The Forerunner*, Al-Mustafa considers his followers as his brothers.

In 1934, *The Garden of the Prophet*, a sequel to *The Prophet*, was published. It tells of the arrival of Al-Mustafa on his island home. At the moment of Gibran's death, the book was in draft form, but according to Barbara Young the guiding principle was still missing. She allowed herself to add several passages which the author may well have intended to use differently. Whereas in *The Prophet*, Gibran touched on subjects basically of an earthly nature and based his twenty-five speeches on moral foundations, in this work he raises metaphysical questions like God, Being and Death. Al-Mustafa declares to his disciples,

You are spirits though you move in bodies, and like oil that burns in the dark, you are the flames though held in lamps. If you were naught save bodies, then my standing before you and speaking unto you would be but emptiness, even as the dead calling unto the dead. But this is not so. All that is deathless in you is free unto the day and the night and cannot be housed nor fettered, for this is the will of the Most High. You are His breath even as the wind that shall be neither caught nor caged. And I also am the breath of His breath.

In that same year, *The King and the Shepherd*, a sketch telling the story of a king who became a shepherd and went to live in the middle of his forests and prairies, was published in Arabic. It was first printed in the biography that Naimy wrote about Gibran. His biography elicited outrage from the friends of the artist, not least of all Amin Rihani. Rihani was offended because 'Mischa' had seen fit to make certain insinuations about Gibran in the belief that the image of Gibran needed a more human dimension; he thought his character had become too mythical when he was still alive.

In 1973, one of the relatives of the artist, his namesake Kahlil, published *Lazarus and His Beloved*, a one-act play found among the manuscripts Mariana had kept for him. In 1981 another unknown play entitled *The Blind* appeared.[1] Undoubtedly inspired by Blake, the creator of a painting entitled *Lazarus*, Gibran tried to imagine Lazarus's state of mind on the morning after his resurrection. For him Lazarus was the only man who knew life twice, death twice, and eternity twice. In his opinion, this character probably did not want to return to life; he was happy beside his heavenly beloved (once again, like the Sufis, earthly love and heavenly love were confused) together

---

1. Unpublished documents found in Knopf's archives show evidence of five one-act plays written by Gibran in English, among which were *Lazarus* and *The Blind*. Following Witter Bynner's advice (from an unpublished letter dated 18 February 1964), Knopf decided not to publish them.

in the heart of God. Convinced he had been sacrificed similarly to the way Jesus had sacrificed himself, he rebelled against the action of his Master.

> 'Why should I be the only one of all the shepherds to be sent back to the desert after knowing green pastures?' [Lazarus asks bitterly.] 'Jesus of Nazareth, tell me now, why did you do this to me? Why did you bring me back to this world when you knew you were going to leave it? Why did you call me back from the heart of eternity to this nightmare?'
>
> 'A miracle was needed. The master brought you back to us so that we would know there was no veil between death and life,' said Marie. 'Don't you realize that you are a living witness to immortality? Don't you see how one single word pronounced with love can gather all the elements dispersed by an illusion called death?'

In her book on Gibran, Barbara Young included some of the previously unpublished writings of the author, such as 'The Blind Poet', 'Ready am I to Go' and 'Jesus Knocking at the Gate of Heaven'. As for the Gibran Museum, it houses unpublished texts that contain illuminating reflections on art, knowledge and beauty, religion and fanaticism.

All the posthumous publications and the unpublished texts which have been exhumed do not overshadow the burning question: is Gibran a man of one single book? Surely not, as the body of work he wrote in Arabic and his prolific texts in English contain many beautiful pieces. Though even if Gibran is remembered solely for one book, would he have minded? He himself wrote to his beloved Mary, towards the end of his life, 'I came into this world to write a book, a single little book.'

In fact, Gibran is more than a writer. He is a 'case'. During his life, he thirsted for political, social, and metaphysical freedom. Driven by a rebellious streak, he wrote, 'Life without revolt is like seasons without spring in the desert.' Having a deep sense for understanding human concerns, he denounced injustice and oppression and relentlessly defended the rights of women in the East.

> Are you a husband who allows for himself things that he disallows for his wife, living in abandonment with the key of her prison in his boots, gorging himself with his favorite food while she sits, by herself, before an empty dish? Or are you a companion, taking no action except hand in hand, nor doing anything unless she gives her thoughts and opinions, and sharing with her your happiness and success? If you are the first, then you are the remnant of a tribe which, still dressing in the skins of animals, vanished long before leaving the caves; and if you are the second, then you are a leader in a nation moving in the dawn toward the light of justice and wisdom.[1]

Motivated by an inspiration that it would be no exaggeration to call divine, Gibran preached love, brotherhood and hope, thereby becoming a spiritual leader for many. He also infused new blood into Arabic literature: with his drive and the impetus of some of his contemporaries, the Arabic language was revamped. It gained flexibility and clarity, and it loosened itself from the yoke that constrained it. In doing so, he imposed himself as one of the most significant reformers of the *nahda*, the renaissance of Arabic culture, and one of the precursors of modern Arabic at the end of the 1950s. Were there really two Gibrans, one a rebel and the other spiritual? One worldly and the other mystical? Although some writers have tried to support this thesis, the theory does not hold water. In essence, the itinerary of Gibran's thought seems very coherent, and his juxtaposition of ideas or different attitudes was not contradictory, but rather a paradox. For him, the various elements melted into one

---

1.   Extract from 'The New Frontier'.

perfect unity. Where is Gibran today? He will come back, no doubt, as he promised to the people of Orphalese. He has, in the image of his God, fused with the storm, the wind, and the trees ... And when, up there, in Bsharri, the fires go out and the moon, open like an eye, lights up, don't we think we hear in the shepherd's nay saluting the stars, the bewitching voice of the Prophet?

Acknowledgments

I would like to thank the National Committee of Gibran, Wahib Keyrouz, curator of the Gibran Museum, Katia Médawar of the American University of Beirut, Afifé Arsanios, former Lebanese Cultural Attaché in Washington, Mr Hyam Mallat, former president of the National Archives of Lebanon, and the poets and journalists Abbas Beydoun, Abdo Wazen and Henri Zogheib, for the works and documents to which they gave me access. I also thank Hind Darwish for her support and Beth Moore of the Telfair Museum of Art in Savannah for her kind cooperation.

Bibliography

Works by Gibran in Arabic

Al-Mussiqa (On Music), New York: Al-Mohajer, 1905.

'Ara'is al-Muruj (Nymphs of the Valley), New York: Al-Mohajer, 1906.

Al-Arwah al-Mutamarrida (Spirits Rebellious), New York: Al-Mohajer, 1908.

Al-Ajniha al-Mutakassira (Broken Wings), New York: Mir'at al-Gharb, 1912.

Dam'a wa ibtisama (A Tear and A Smile), New York: Mir'at al-Gharb, 1914.

Al-Mawakib (The Processions), New York: Mir'at al-Gharb, 1919.

Al-'Awasif (The Tempests), Cairo: Al-Hilal, 1920.

Al-Badai' wal Tara'if (Wonders and Curiosities), Cairo: Yusuf Bustani, al-Matba'a al-assriya, 1923.

Kalimat Gibran (Spiritual Sayings), edited by Antonios Bachir, Cairo, 1927; Beirut: Dar al-Mutahida, 1983.

Works by Gibran in English

The Madman: His Parables and Poems, New York: Alfred A. Knopf, 1918; London: Heinemann, 1946.

The Forerunner: His Parables and Poems, New York: Alfred A. Knopf, 1920; London: Heinemann, 1963.

The Prophet, New York: Alfred A. Knopf, 1923; London: Heinemann, 1926.

Sand and Foam, New York: Alfred A. Knopf, 1926; London: Heinemann, 1927.

Jesus, the Son of Man: His Words and His Deeds as Told and Recorded by Those Who Knew Him, New York: Alfred A. Knopf, 1928; London: Heinemann, 1954; Oxford: Oneworld, 1993.

The Earth Gods, New York: Alfred A. Knopf, 1931; London: Heinemann, 1962.

The Wanderer: His Parables and his Sayings, New York: Alfred A. Knopf, 1932; London: Heinemann, 1965.

The Garden of the Prophet, New York: Alfred A. Knopf, 1933; London: Heinemann, 1954.

Lazarus and His Beloved: A One-Act Play, Greenwich, Connecticut: New York Graphic Society, 1973; London: Heinemann, 1973; Philadelphia: Westminster Press, 1982.

The Blind, Greenwich, Connecticut: New York Graphic Society, 1981; Philadelphia: Westminster Press, 1982.

Gibran's works of art

Twenty Drawings, intro. A. Raphael, New York: Alfred A. Knopf, 1919.

Works by Gibran translated from Arabic

Broken Wings, trans. A. R. Ferris, New York: Citadel Press, 1957, 1989; London: Heinemann, 1959; New York: Wisdom Library, 1972.

Nymphs of the Valley, trans. H. M. Nahmad, New York: Alfred A. Knopf, 1948; London: Heinemann, 1948.

Spirits Rebellious, trans. H. M. Nahmad, New York: Alfred A. Knopf, 1948; London: Heinemann, 1949, 1964.

A Tear and a Smile, trans. H. M. Nahmad, intro. R. Hillyer, New York: Alfred A. Knopf, 1950, 1994; London: Heinemann, 1950.

Tears and Laughter, trans. A. R. Ferris, New York: Philosophical Library, 1947; New York: First Carol, 1990.

Anthologies and Collected Works

The Beloved: Reflections on the Path of the Heart, trans. J. Walbridge, Ashland: White Cloud Press, 1994.

Between Night and Morn: A Special Selection, trans. A. R. Ferris, New York: Wisdom Library, 1972.

The Collected Works, New York: Everyman's Library, Alfred A Knopf, 2007.

The Eye of the Prophet, trans. M. Crosland, London: Souvenir Press, 1995.

Kahlil Gibran: A spiritual treasury, ed. Suheil Bushrui, Oxford: Oneworld, 2001.

The Khalil Gibran Reader: Inspirational Writings, Secaucus: Carol Publishing Group, 1995.

The Life of Khalil Gibran and his Procession, trans. G. Khairallah, New York: Arab-American Press, 1947; New York: Wisdom Library, 1958.

Mirrors of the Soul, trans. J. Sheban, New York: Philosophical Library, 1965; New York: First Carol, 1992.

Oeuvres Complètes, Robert Laffont, Paris: Coll. Bouquins, 2006.

Prophecies of Love: Reflections from the Heart, ed. J. Clardy, Kansas City: Hallmark Cards Inc., 1971.

Prose Poems, trans. A. Ghareeb, New York: Alfred A. Knopf, 1934; London: Heinemann, 1964.

A Second Treasury of Khalil Gibran, trans. A. R. Ferris, New York: Citadel Press, 1962.

Secrets of the Heart, trans. A. R. Ferris, New York: Philosophical Library, 1947; New York: Signet, 1965; New York: First Carol, 1992.

Spirit Brides, trans. J. Cole, Santa Cruz: White Cloud Press, 1993.

Spiritual Sayings, trans. A. R. Ferris, New York: Bantam, 1970; London: Heinemann, 1962, 1974.

The Storm: Stories and poems, trans. J. Walbridge, Santa Cruz: White Cloud Press, 1993.

A Third Treasury of Khalil Gibran, Secaucus: Citadel Press, 1975.

Thoughts and Meditations, trans. A. R. Ferris, New York: Citadel Press, 1961; London: Heinemann, 1960, 1961, 1973.

A Treasury of Khalil Gibran, trans. A. R. Ferris, New York: Citadel Press, 1951; London: Heinemann, 1974; London: Mandarin, 1991, 1994.

The Treasured Writings of Khalil Gibran, Secaucus: Castle Books, 1985.

The Vision: Reflections on the Way of the Soul, trans. J. Cole, Ashland: White Cloud Press, 1994.

Visions of the Prophet, trans. Margaret Crosland, London: Souvenir Press, 1996.

The Voice of Khalil Gibran, ed. R. Waterfield, London: Penguin, 1995.

The Voice of the Master, trans. A. R. Ferris, New York: Citadel Press, 1963; London: Heinemann, 1960, 1973.

The Wisdom of Gibran: Aphorisms and Maxims, trans. J. Sheban, New York: Philosophical Library, 1966.

Archives

International Conference on Kahlil Gibran, University of Kaslik, April 3–5, 2006.

International Conference on Kahlil Gibran, University of Maryland, December 1999–January 2000.

Chapel Hill Papers (Minis family papers), Southern Historical Collection, University of North Carolina at Chapel Hill.

Witter Bynner Papers, New Mexico State University, Rio Grande Historical Collections.

Alfred A. Knopf Papers, Harry Ransom Humanities Research Centre, University of Texas, Austin.

Gibran Museum collection and archives, Bsharri, Lebanon.

An-Nahar archives.

Al-Hayat archives.

As-Safir archives.

L'Orient-Le Jour archives.

National Archives, Lebanon.

Telfair Museum of Art collection, Savannah.

Collections of letters

Bushrui, Suheil, and Kuzbari, Salma H., *Love Letters*, Oxford: Oneworld, 1983.

Blue Flame: The Love Letters of Kahlil Gibran and May Ziadah, Harlow: Longman, 1983.

Ferris, Anthony, *A Self-portrait*, New York: Citadel Press, 1959.

Hilu, Virginia, *Beloved Prophet: The Love Letters of Kahlil Gibran and Mary Haskell and her Private Journal*, New York: Alfred A. Knopf, 1972.

Honein, Riad, *Rassa'il Gibran al ta'iha*, Beirut: Naufal, 1983.

Jabre, Jamil, *Rassael Gibran*, Dar Beirut, 1951.

Najjar, Alexandre, *Awraq Gibraniya*, Beirut: Dar An-Nahar, 2006.

Peabody, Josephine Preston, *Diary and letters*, ed. Christina Hopkinson Baker, Boston: 1924.

Salem Otto, Annie, *The Love Letters of Kahlil Gibran and Mary Haskell*, Houston: Annie Salem Otto, 1964.

Unpublished Gibran Letters to Ameen Rihani, trans. S. B. Bushrui, Beirut: Rihani House for the World Lebanese Cultural Union, 1972.

Unpublished letters to Helena Ghostine.

Books and articles about Gibran

Abbud, Marun, *Judud wa qudama*, Beirut: Dar al-Thaqafa, 1st ed. 1954, 2nd ed. 1963.

—— *Mujadidun wa mujtarrun*, Beirut: Dar Marun Abbud/Dar al-Thaqafa, 1st ed. 1948; 5th ed. 1979.

Adonis, Introduction to *Le Prophète*, Folio Classique, no. 2335, Paris: Gallimard, 1992.

Attwe, Fawzi, *Gibran Khalil Gibran*, Beirut: Dar al-fikr al-arabi, 1989.

Boulos, Mitri Selim, *Alghaz Gibraniya*, Beirut : Agate, 2001.

—— Boustani, Fouad Ephrem, *Maa Gibran*, Beirut: 1983.

—— *Gibran bayna al jassad wal ruh*, Beirut: al-Da'ira, 2003.

Braks, Ghazi, *Gibran Khalil Gibran*, Beirut: Dar al-Kitab al-Lubnani, 1981.

Bushrui, Suheil, 'Gibran, le Prophète du Liban', in *Le Magazine Littéraire*, no. 359, November 1997.

—— *Kahlil Gibran, A Survey of His Life and His Work*, Ibadan: Ibadan University Press, 1966.

—— *Kahlil Gibran of Lebanon*, Gerrards Cross: Colin Smythe, 1987.

Bushrui, Suheil, and Jenkins, Joe, *Kahlil Gibran, Man and poet*, Oxford-Boston: Oneworld, 1998.

Ceccatty, René de, 'Khalil Gibran, les prophéties d'un esthète', in *Le Monde*, 19 February 1999.

Chahine, Anis, *L'amour et la nature dans l'œuvre de Khalil Gibran*, Beirut: Middle East Press, 1979.

Chalfun, Khalil, *La figure de Jésus-Christ dans la vie et l'œuvre de Gibran Khalil Gibran*, PhD thesis, Paris: Institut Catholique, 1986.

Chikhani, Rafic, *Religion et société dans l'œuvre de Gibran Khalil Gibran*, PhD thesis, Strasbourg, 1983; Beirut: Lebanese University, 1997.

Chueiri, Raja, *Bsharri, Gibran et le gibranisme*, Beirut: Félix Beryte Publishers, 1999.

Collective, *Khalil Gibran and Amin Rihani, prophets of Lebanese-American Literature*, Louaize: Notre Dame University, 1999.

Comeir, Youhanna, *Gibran wa Nietzsche*, Beirut: Naufal, 1997.

Dahdah, Jean-Pierre, 'Khalil Gibran, poète de la sagesse', in *Question De*, no. 83, Paris : Albin Michel, 1990.

—— *Khalil Gibran: une biographie*, Paris: Albin Michel, 1994; pocket edition, 2004.

—— *Dictionnaire de l'oeuvre de Khalil Gibran*, Paris: Dervy, 2007.

Daye, Jean, *Aqidat Gibran*, London: Sourakia House, 1988.

Francis, Antoine, *Gibran al-Achiq*, Beirut: Dar As-Sayad, 1987.

Ghaith, Afifa, *La pensée religieuse chez Gibran Khalil Gibran et Mikhaïl Nuayma*, Louvain: Peeters Press, 1990.

Ghougassian, J.-P, *Khalil Gibran: L'envol de l'esprit*, Quebec: Mortagne, 1986.

Ghraizi, Wafic, *Nissa'on fi hayati Gibran*, Beirut: Dar Al-Taliaa, 1982.

Gibran, Khalil and Jean, *Kahlil Gibran. His Life and Works*, New York: Interlink Books, 1st ed. 1974; 2nd ed. 1981.

—— Introduction to *Dramas of life: Lazarus and his beloved and The Blind*, Philadelphia: Westminster Press, 1982.

Habib, Boutros, *Jadaliat al hub wal mawt fi mu'allifat Gibran*, Beirut, 1995.

Hage, George Nicolas, *William Blake and Kahlil Gibran*, Binghamton: State University of New York, 1980; Louaize: Notre Dame University, 2002.

Hatem, Jad, *La mystique de Gibran et le Supra-confessionnalisme religieux des chrétiens d'Orient*, Paris: Deux Océans, 1999.

Hawi, Khalil, *Khalil Gibran: His Background, Character and Works*, Beirut: American University of Beirut, 1963.

Helou, Joseph Habib, *Kahlil Gibran a Nonpareil artist*, Beirut, 2002.

Honein, Riad, *al-wajh al akhar li Gibran*, Beirut: Dar an-Nahar, 1981.

Huwayyik, Yusuf, *Gibran in Paris*, New York: Popular Library, 1976.

Jabre, Jamil, *Gibran fi hayatihi al assifa*, Beirut: Naufal, 1981.

—— *Gibran*, Beirut: Naufal, 1983.

Karam, Antoine Ghattas, *La vie et l'œuvre littéraire de Gibran Khalil Gibran*, Beirut: Dar an-Nahar, 1981; 2nd ed. 2005 (intro. A. Najjar).

Kayruz, Wahib, *Gibran dans son musée*, Bacharia, 1996.

—— *La dialectique unificatrice dans la pensée de Gibran*, Bacharia, 1983.

Aalam Gibran al fikri, 2 vols, Bacharia, 1984.

—— *La Procession de la Matrice Vierge* (entretiens), Le Pinacle de Beirut, 1999.

Khaled, Amin, *Muhawalat fi darsi Gibran*, Beirut: Imprimerie catholique, 1933.

Kharrat, Souad, *Gibran le prophète, Nietzsche le visionnaire*, Triptyque, 1993.

Khueiry, Antoine, *Gibran Khalil Gibran: al nabigha al lubnani*, Beirut, 1981.

Khury, Raïf Georges, *Passé et présent de la culture arabe, Tradition, modernité et conservation d'identité selon Gibran*, Neckarhausen: Ed. des Deux Mondes, 1997.

Knopf, Alfred A., *Portrait of a Publisher, 1915–1965: Reminiscences and Reflections*, 2 vols, New York: The Typophiles, 1965.

Maalouf, Amin, 'Introduction to *Le Prophète*', Le Livre de Poche, no. 9685, 1993.

Maalouf, Ruchdi, *Gibran Khalil Gibran*, Cénacle libanais, no. 10–11, 1948.

Massoud, Habib, *Gibran hayan wa maytan*, Dar Al-Rihani, 2nd ed. 1966.

Naaman, Abdallah, 'Du côté du 14 avenue du Maine (Gibran à Paris)', in *Arabies*, October 1993.

—— *Histoire des Orientaux de France*, Paris: Ellipses, 2004.

Naimy, Mikhaïl, *Gibran Khalil Gibran*, 1934.

—— *Kahlil Gibran: A Biography*, New York: Philosophical Library, 1950.

—— *Sab'oun* (in Arabic), Beirut: Naufal, 1977–8.

Naimy, Nadim, *The Lebanese Prophets of New York*, Beirut: American University of Beirut, 1985.

Najjar, Alexandre, *Khalil Gibran*, Pygmalion, 2002; J'ai Lu, 2006.

—— 'Unpublished letters of Gibran', in *Al-Hayat*, December 2005.

—— 'Gibran in Paris', Exhibition Catalogue, Paris Book Fair, Lebanese Ministry of Culture (22–27 March 2002).

—— *Dictionary Gibran*, Beirut: Dar Al-Saqi, 2008

Norin, Luc, *Autour de Khalil Gibran*, La Renaissance du Livre, 2002.

Salem, Otto Annie, *The Parables of Kahlil Gibran; an interpretation of his writings and his Art*, New York: Citadel Press, 1963.

Sayegh, Toufic, *Adwa jadida ala Gibran*, London: Riad Rayyes Books, 2nd ed. 1990.

Shehadi, Walid, *A Prophet in the making*, Beirut: American University of Beirut, 1991.

Sherfan, Andrew Dib, *Khalil Gibran: The Nature of Love*, New York: Philosophical Library, 1971.

Stétié, Salah, Introduction to *Le Prophète*, La Renaissance du Livre, 1998.

Tawk, Boulos, *La Personnalité de Gibran dans ses dimensions constitutives et existentielles*, PhD thesis, Strasbourg, 1984; Bacharia, 1985 (3 vols).

Wade, Minkowski Anne, 'Un autre Gibran', in *Le Prophète*, Gallimard, Folio Classique, no. 2335, 1992.

Waterfield, Robin, *Prophet: The Life and Times of Kahlil Gibran*, Penguin Press, 1998.

Yammouni, Joseph, *Gibran Khalil Gibran: l'homme et sa pensée philosophique*, Lausanne: Ed. de l'Aire, 1982.

Young, Barbara: *This Man from Lebanon: A study of Khalil Gibran*, New York: Alfred A. Knopf, 1945.

Zacca, Najib, *Littérature libanaise contemporaine*, Université Saint-Esprit de Kaslik, 2002.

Zogheib, Henri, 'Le phénomène Gibran aux Etats-Unis', in *Arabies*, October 1993.

—— '*Maa Gibran fi Marjhine*', in *An-Nahar*, 15 and 17 October 2001.

About Gibran's paintings

Kayrouz, Wahib, *Aalam Gibran al rassam*, Lebanon: 1982.

Sultan, Fayçal, *Gibran le peintre*, in *L'Orient-Le Jour*, 6, 11, 13 and 15 May 1981.

Tarrab, Joseph, *Khalil Gibran, horizons du peintre*, Beirut: Les Documents de l'Agenda culturel, 2000.

Khalil Gibran, horizons of the painter, Nicolas-Sursock Museum (Exhibition catalogue 17 December 1999–31 January 2000).

Khalil Gibran, artiste et visionnaire, Institut du Monde Arabe/Flammarion, 1998.

About Fred Holland Day

Jussim, Estelle, *Slave to Beauty: The Eccentric and Controversial Career of F. Holland Day*, Boston: David R. Godine, 1981.

Parrish, S. M., *Currents of the Nineties in Boston and London: Fred Holland Day, Louise Imogen Guiney and their Circle*, New York: Garland, 1987.

Roberts, Pam (ed.), *F. Holland Day*, Amsterdam: Van Gogh Museum, 2001.

About May Ziadeh

Boulos, Mitri Selim, *Gibran wa May bayna al khayal wal waqeh*, Beirut: Agate, 2001.

Ghorayeb, Rose, *May Ziadé*, Naufal, 1978.

Jabre, Jamil, *May wa Gibran*, Beirut: 1950.

—— *May wa Gibran: qissat hob*, Sader, 2001.

Kouzbary, Salwa Haffar, *May Ziadé*, 2 vols, Naufal, 1987.

Index

Page numbers followed by 'ft' indicate a footnote.